# How to Change Other People:
# The Self-Discovery Solution

### By

### Jayne Gardner, Ph.D.

ISBN: 1-40331-849-2 (e-book)
ISBN: 1-40331-850-6 (Paperback)

Library of Congress Control Number: 2002091224


This book is printed on acid free paper.


Printed in the United States of America
Bloomington, IN


1stBooks - rev. 07/16/02

In order to ensure the privacy and medical confidentiality of certain individuals mentioned in this book names, places, and other identifying details concerning those individuals have been changed.

*Do not judge, or you too will be judged. For in the same way you judge others, you will be judged, and with the measure you use, it will be measured to you.*

*Why do you look at the speck of sawdust in your brother's eye and pay no attention to the plank in your own eye? How can you say to your brother, "Let me take the speck out of your eye," when all the time there is a plank in your own eye? You hypocrite, first take the plank out of your own eye, and then you will see clearly to remove the speck from your own brother's eye.*

*Matthew 7: 1-6*

# Acknowledgments

Many people have touched my life in a positive way during the writing of this book and I am grateful for all their true selves. But, David, I am amazed you always saw the true me and your love and support are witness to your God within. Thank you for loving both my True Self and my False Self. Thank you to my four children and my Mother and my Father for understanding my need to share our personal lives. Thanks to Melissa for reading and typing my notes but mostly for continuing to challenge my False Self to publish this story. I am grateful for the example set by the plaintiffs in the lawsuit. Thank you to my personal coach, Alisa Garber, whose steadiness has kept me on course. This book could not have been written without the courage of my clients who shared their stories. The Discovery Group members have continually validated the program's value. Monica Ramirez Basco offered me support through the long months of writing and publishing. My Assistant, Debi's loyalty has been heartwarming. Thanks to Reverend Carol Record, Linda Taylor, Christopher Ian Chenoweth and my friends at Unity Church who also believe God is on the inside.

To my first readers, Gayla and Mike Hope, Ben and Lori Cohen, Mary Lenn Dixon, Judy Crow, Jane Hickerson, Jayne Wakeham, and Carolyn David - I appreciate you holding a space for me. Thanks to editors Mary Jo Beebe and Harry Roth for their hours of editing. Blessings to the many typists who have valiantly read my handwriting: Kara, Toni, Joanne, Kristi, Dana and others. Thanks to Arnie and Marian for always inquiring about the book's progress and never losing faith in me. My dear friends, Bill and Di for all the rest and rejuvenation at their home in Florida, I am grateful.

# Table of Contents

INTRODUCTION: EVERYTHING BEGINS WITH YOU............................................................. xiii

PART I: BECOMING AWARE OF A FALSE SELF AND A TRUE SELF ............................................. 1

CHAPTER ONE: LIVING ON THE OUTSIDE .. 3

Self-Discovery Dialogue One......................... 16

CHAPTER TWO: TURNING AROUND TO LOOK INSIDE .............................................. 30

Self-Discovery Dialogue Two ........................ 38

CHAPTER THREE: PROTECTING MYSELF . 53

Self- Discovery Dialogue Three .................... 68

PART II: RECOGNIZING THE DIFFERENCE BETWEEN THE FALSE SELF AND THE TRUE SELF ...................................................... 82

CHAPTER FOUR: IDENTIFYING MYSELF ... 84

Self-Discovery Dialogue Four ........................ 97

CHAPTER FIVE: GROWING MYSELF UP ... 111

Self-Discovery Dialogue Five....................... 120

CHAPTER SIX: FORGIVING MYSELF ......... 131

Self-Discovery Dialogue Six ........................ 143

PART III: DEVELOPING A RELATIONSHIP BETWEEN YOUR FALSE SELF AND YOUR TRUE SELF........................................................ 157

CHAPTER SEVEN: PUMPING UP MY TRUE SELF ............................................................. 159

Self-Discovery Dialogue Seven.................... 167

CHAPTER EIGHT: CHANGING OF THE

GUARD .......................................................... 187

Self-Discovery Dialogue Eight.............................. 198

CHAPTER NINE: FINDING THE GOD

WITHIN.......................................................... 210

Self-Discovery Dialogue Nine...................... 224

AFTERWORD ........................................................ 234

DEFINITION OF TERMS ...................................... 243

REFERENCES ...................................................... 247

# Introduction:

## Everything Begins with You

Life can be painful.  Relationships can be difficult. If you are reading this, you may know first hand what I am talking about.  You may have worked very hard, in a relationship, to make things better, only to find it hasn't worked.  This book is offered to make you aware of a different way to change the people you love. By discovering, acknowledging, and accessing your own power, and being the first to change, you can model change.  What I hope you will discover is: Everything Begins with You. You have the power within you and it is far more powerful than you ever imagined.

The process and concepts presented in this book provide a methodology related to a new science, Spiritual Psychology, which deals with the human spirit in much the same way traditional psychology studies the personality. Spiritual Psychology is primarily focused on the relationship we have with ourselves.

The strength of the relationship we have with ourselves has a direct bearing on how others relate to us as individuals. This book will focus on connecting you with your True Self.

The process of connecting with your True Self and the development of your soul is divided into nine dialogues, which I call The Self-Discovery Solution. Each dialogue is a writing assignment that leads you along the path of uncovering and developing your True Self. To discover who you really are you will need to:

1. Become aware of both your False Self and True Self. (Part I, Dialogues 1-3)

2. Recognize the difference between the two in your written and spoken inner dialogue. (Part II, Dialogues 4-6)

3. Develop a continuing relationship between your False Self and your True Self. (Part III, Dialogues 7-9)

I use the terminology False Self when referring to the personality and True Self when referring to the soul/higher self. I use the word dialogue in this book to mean the continuing conversation between your personality (False Self) and your highest self (True Self), which is going on in your head all the time.

What I want for you is a relationship with your highest being, your True Self. This is the highest essence of your human spirit, your soul. My wish is that through telling my story, you will discover a loving relationship within yourself.

What I also want for you is to come to know that changing other people is possible in a new and positive way, by learning to love and accept your highest self, the God within.

---

*Everything begins with you.*

---

# Part I:

# Becoming Aware of a False

# Self and a True Self

Chapters 1, 2 & 3

*Jayne Gardner, Ph.D.*

# Chapter One:

# Living on the Outside

---

*A significant emotional event is an opportunity for*

*self-discovery and personal growth.*

---

*Self-understanding and acceptance of the bond we form with ourselves is in many ways the most crucial challenge we face.*

*Caroline Myss*

*That morning in February, the darkest time of the year, I parked in the gloom of early morning. Light was beginning to clear away the shadows of night, but the blackness lingered. I turned off the engine and* stared through the windshield at the huge church. I could see the cathedral spires against the pale morning sky. For just a moment, I wondered what would happen when I met with the minister, a town celebrity. I checked my makeup in the rear-view mirror and reapplied lipstick to my carefully lined lips.

My life was a mess, and that meant I was a mess. I just didn't know it. After all, I had a doctorate in counseling and was diligently working on my "issues." But my husband of twenty-plus years and I were separating, so I sought spiritual guidance from the pastor of a church near where I lived. Several people I respected had read his books and liked his more liberal interpretations of the Bible. My faith in God needed shoring up, and I figured that I could get a booster shot of faith from someone as wise as he was supposed to be. I had no idea how God related to the mess I was in, but some small voice in me told me to find out. I eagerly anticipated our meeting and looked forward to a solution to my problems.

I decided it would be okay to go in, although I was early. It seemed too dark and too early in the morning for a professional meeting. But this man of God said he was available for an early morning meeting only, and I was eager to please him. Although my day was tightly scheduled with patients, I adjusted my schedule to fit his. That was my first mistake.

I locked my car door and quickly walked to the dark side entrance. I could see the sun rising on the other side, but the shadows on my side of the building swallowed me. I didn't know if anyone was in the church yet. There were no other cars in the parking *lot.  I thought that a high-profile man with his own televised church service was probably chauffeured to work or parked in his own private space. He was, after all, senior minister of one of the largest Protestant churches in the country.  But I was only guessing. I had no idea about the lifestyle of someone so powerful.*

*Thinking about his status and position made me nervous. I had heard about him all my life because I had been brought up in the same denomination, and my uncle, our family's best and brightest, was a minister also. I knew he would be pleased that I'd sought help from our town's most popular minister.*

*Now I had a chance to explain my situation and sorrow to a wise person recognized in the Christian world as an authority on such matters. I pushed aside* the nervousness of confiding in a stranger by reassuring myself with my family's opinion of him.

The side entrance was open, so I went in. Once more I was swallowed by shadows, as if the darkness was trying to warn me of what was to come. Another person might have been scared in such a huge, dark building, but growing up in the church meant that for me the familiar space felt safe, like the sanctuary it was. I was reminded of my grandmother's advice when I was a child: you can always find the light on in your pastor's study in time of need. Unafraid, I walked through the church looking for that light.

I found the women's restroom instead and ducked in to make sure I looked all right. I surveyed myself in the full-length mirror and felt I was suitable for the *meeting. I looked good on the outside even if my insides were a bit squeamish.*

*Eventually I found the business office. Because of the early hour, I wasn't surprised that the secretary wasn't there. For a moment I wondered at the meeting's clandestine character, but I quickly dismissed any fear. The minister knew my uncle, I reminded myself. Being generous with his time was just a professional courtesy. But I was flattered by the meeting's intimacy.*

*"Good morning," boomed the minister.*

*His presence stopped my ruminating. Suddenly, we were standing face to face. His voice sounded as strong and as powerful as God's voice might sound, and I felt at ease with him immediately. I followed him like a disciple down the hall. I was glad I had dressed well; I could tell by his glance that he approved of my looks.*

*We had to pass through two offices before we reached his secluded study. Because of the privacy, the study seemed protected, a sacred place. Dark red drapes covered the tall windows, allowing no outside view. Bookcases lined one side of the office, and a small seating arrangement stood in front of the minister's massive wooden desk. The room suited him perfectly—private and sophisticated.*

*I wanted him to know that I was a follower. I walked over to the books immediately and bantered about his writings and his television broadcasts. I was avoiding my purpose in coming, and he seemed to know that. He did not waste time with pleasantries and invited me to sit with him on the sofa. He wanted to know why I had come.*

*His inquiry reminded me of what I always say to my own clients in therapy. I liked the role reversal. I felt calmed, even relieved not to have to be the helper. I relaxed into the sofa and began my story.*

*I was in the throes of a separation from my childhood sweetheart, the man I had been married to for twenty-four years. I was passionately in love with another man and just as deeply filled with remorse and guilt. I had decided to tell my husband, but I felt nauseated by the grief it would cause him. I knew the thoughts were wrong, yet I couldn't seem to find my usual self-discipline. I felt very needy, like a child seeking forgiveness.*

*I told him how I'd felt verbally abused and unloved for many years in my long, difficult marriage. I told him I had been faithful previously but now was having thoughts of infidelity. I know my cheeks must have burned with embarrassment, but if I could not be honest here, then where?*

*He asked me about my sex life with my husband. I told him about it, even though I knew that was not the reason for my unhappiness. However, he was very interested in the sexual part of our relationship, and at first I thought he was questioning me from a therapeutic perspective. Because I assumed he was an expert, I willingly opened up and answered all his questions about my very private life.*

*As he probed, I felt embarrassed and realized I was ignoring the objections of my inner voice. I never asked for such detail about a client's sex life in the first interview. Still, I allowed him to ask detailed questions about mine because I was intent on letting him decide what was relevant. On some level, I knew I was abdicating responsibility for myself. By not listening to my inner voice, I was unconsciously abandoning myself.*

*During the conversation, I kept my eyes averted as my answers to his questions divulged more and more intimate details. When I was finally able to look up into his eyes, he moved closer.*

*I wanted so much to have his approval and ultimate forgiveness. I had placed him on a pedestal and shrouded him with divinity. I was convinced that his position, his power, and his words could heal me.*

*Instead, when I looked up into his face, I saw his dark, shadowy self.*

*His seduction surprised me, but my reaction to his sexual invitation surprised me even more. I felt helpless at his touch and flattered he was attracted to me. I had been taught to worship and obey authority figures, especially men of God, and so felt powerless. He murmured that he thought he had found his soul mate in me. The wise part of me knew the foolishness and manipulation of such a statement, but a more needy part wanted it to be true. I felt unable to tell him to stop. I was bewildered and had lost the natural instinct to protect myself.*

*Some part of me had seen the seduction coming with the line of sexual questioning. For someone I had known for all of ten minutes to ask me about the intimate details of my sexual life was highly inappropriate and invasive. Then I remembered my warning thoughts about the early hour he had scheduled the appointment and the darkness and seclusion of his office.*

*My willingness to trust an external authority based solely on his status led me into a betrayal of my True Self. My total lack of regard for my internal warnings about his questions had weakened me. I allowed myself to be victimized by his seduction because I did not trust myself, my own inner authority. I was so very needy of some outside source to fix my life.*

*He misinterpreted my silence for acquiescence and for a few seconds I relinquished my dignity to please this man of God. It took about the same amount of time to run from his office, down the hallway, and out into the early morning light.*

Part of me wanted to forget the incident. I tried to go about my daily life, seeing clients and taking care of my family. Somewhere inside me a voice told me to start keeping a journal.

A client brought in a copy of <u>The Artists Way</u> by Julia Cameron. While I had journaled before, the method of morning writing outlined in her book was particularly useful for me. I got up early every morning and wrote for thirty minutes. My self-discovery process had begun.

*You're on the verge of creative movement. Just go with it. You cannot be fixed in how you're going about it any more than you could be fixed if you were setting about to paint a great work of art.  Be alert.  Be self-aware so that when opportunity presents itself, you can actually rise to it.*

*David Bohm in Joseph Jaworski's <u>Synchronicity</u>*

Join me now in the first step toward self-discovery. To find your True Self, I direct you inward to complete Dialogue One.

### <u>Self-Discovery Dialogue One</u>

Listening to your inner voice

*The only journey is the one within.*

*Rainer Maria Rilke*

To find your inner voice, your link to your True Self, begin journaling your thoughts and feelings every morning. Your journal will become an inner stage where two actors will emerge, your True Self and your False Self. The earlier you start writing in the morning, the easier it is to overhear the dialogue constantly going on in your head. This writing will be the basis for your discovery of your True Self's voice.

"What if I can't hear a dialogue in my head or can't think of anything to write down?" you might ask.

You have answered your own question. Simply write down that one thought. It might be as follows:

*"Okay, so what in the world am I supposed to write down here? I can't understand what she is telling me to do. She might think it*

*sounds easy or that it will be helpful, but I don't know. I really doubt that this is the right thing for me. What possible help could this be? I've kept journals before and nothing changed."*

OR

*"I'd like to try this. It sounds pretty obvious that writing down what's going on in my head would give me knowledge of myself. I'm a little afraid of finding out."*

I am asking you to copy down all the thoughts and feelings running through your head, your internal dialogue. Here are some examples of internal dialogue from some of my clients:

1. *I told myself to work harder on my relationship with Laurie.*

2. *You must quit making so many mistakes.*

3. *You did really well on that special project at the office.*

4. *That person in the restaurant must have thought I was a real slob.*

5. *I have so many things to do today, I'll never get them all done.*

Your writing will never be read by another person, so don't worry about content, grammar, or spelling. Be nonjudgmental of what you overhear and just copy it down, automatically emptying out your own thoughts and feelings on the written page. Listen to yourself, and write down everything you hear. Paper can be a great listener.

Clients came to me in the middle of some life crisis similar to the one that led me to visit the minister. They usually want to work on changing someone else's negative attitudes. The minister was a perfect example of the universal need to focus on changing others instead of working on ourselves. His life work was about saving souls and yet he seemed unaware that his own soul was lost. At that point in my life, I was also focusing on changing others and, like the minister, has chosen a career to fulfill this savior complex. Here's the journal of a woman who's struggling with a crisis in a relationship. Of course, she came to me requesting I help her change her husband's negative attitude toward her.

## Marie's First Journaling for Dialogue One

*She says that I have to escape for 30 minutes every day. Write in a book about what is bottled up inside of me. We have to figure out how I lost myself. My spirituality. My Life Force. I just go through the motions of life. In my little cage, I run my little errands and take my little boy to his appointments. I try to get through a day of feeling happy. Like I belong somehow.*

*But I don't belong. I don't fit in. Angry reminders pop into my brain when I least expect them. There's so many. I have huge resentments about my husband's lack of love for me. I am sad because he never wants to be with me. He is always taking advantage of me. I*

> *have lots and lots of anger. I wonder what happened to all my good feelings? Why do I feel so inadequate? I can't seem to remember the good times in my marriage.*
>
> *If I had to do it all over again, what would I do? I used to think about this all of the time. And it's a depressing thought. I am afraid writing about all these emotions will make me feel worse.*

But instead of feeling worse, just the opposite occurs as you follow-through with your writing every morning. By releasing your negative thoughts, you are acknowledging them. Most likely you have suppressed them to the point where these negative feelings are buried. Some people might tell you that ignoring negative thoughts or feelings will make them go away.

The reverse is actually true. The more you try to repress a negative thought or emotion, the more it will make itself known in your life.

Here's my own journal entry a few weeks after the incident with the minister.

## Author's Journaling for Dialogue #1

*I know I did something horribly wrong. I can't understand why I didn't stand up for myself and tell him off. Why did I freeze? I was so worried about his approval of my appearance. Did I encourage him? What does he think of me now? I'm not planning on telling anyone and I'm sure he won't either. I thought I was doing the right thing by seeking out the conference with someone so powerful. Where was my voice? How could I have given in, even if only for a few seconds? No guts. I should have slapped him. I will call the church and report it. No. I'd better wait. That would not make me look very good. I just remember wanting to please him. And now, I am so angry.*

By writing down my inner dialogue, I began to listen to myself. As you can see, my focus continued to be on changing others.

As you will come to learn, life does not happen to you; you create the happenings of your life by your inner thoughts and feelings. Later in this process, you will find out how to change this inner dialogue and create the life you really want. Right now the purpose of your writing is to become more conscious of your thoughts, to reveal how you are currently creating the reality around you.

As you complete your writing exercises, you will experience both negative and positive feelings about this self-discovery process and your writing. I call the negative feelings <u>resistance</u> and the positive feelings <u>wins</u>. I cannot over-emphasize the importance of each of these, especially your wins, to your personal growth. For that reason, I will call your attention to each of these in every dialogue.

<u>RESISTANCE</u>: To hear your True Self's voice you must set the stage by forming a habit of writing everyday. As soon as you have written for seven days in a row, you can trust yourself to move to Dialogue Two. What will keep you from writing? At some

level, you will realize that finding your True Self's voice will change the choices you make. A part of you will do anything to avoid scrutiny. This False Self is the old unconscious thinking that tells you to be satisfied with the status quo. The False Self is slippery as an eel and will try to sabotage this writing process. It wants to resist change and keep the comfortable familiarity of old ways and thoughts. Push on, knowing you are going in the right direction.

Inside wins are discoveries you have made about yourself as you go through self-discovery. As you work through these dialogues, you will begin to change (your image of yourself).

<u>INSIDE WINS:</u> List three discoveries you've made about yourself in this step:

1.

2.

3.

As you work and focus on yourself, the people around you will begin to change. Outside wins are changes that occur in the outside world and in your relationships with others as a result of the changes you make in yourself. **Realize that any change you observe in others is a result of changes in you.**

OUTSIDE WINS: List three ways your discoveries can change others:

1.

2.

3.

CHECKPOINT: The goal at this point is to just hear and be aware of your internal dialogue. At the end of the week, re-read your writing and notice any consistent attitude or tone in your writing. Do you find any clearly positive or negative tone of voice? Before proceeding to Dialogue Two, make sure you have established the habit of writing every day for at least six or seven days a week. Please repeat Dialogue One until you have this habit firmly entrenched. Then you have taken the first step toward discovering your True Self.

---

*<u>Stay alert</u> for any small or subtle changes in others that indicate your own inner shifts are impacting others. Continue to increase your belief in your power to change others by changing yourself. Keep writing every day.*

---

# Chapter Two:

# Turning Around to Look Inside

*The True Self has been overshadowed by the False Self, which must be brought into our awareness.*

*"Naming something that affects us adversely,"* states Christiane Northrup in <u>Women's Bodies, Women's Wisdom</u>, *"is part of freeing ourselves from its continued influence. Many times healing can not begin until we allow ourselves to feel how bad things are or were in the past."*

Awareness of my False Self gradually came about because of the incident with the minister. Until then, I had not been aware of how much I had become what others wanted me to be. Until this incident happened, I was not aware of living outside myself in a false state of mind. I had always thought of problems happening to me and considered the world doing things both good and bad to me where I had no control over what happened. People and events, I felt, caused me to be either happy or sad.

Gradually, I came to understand this fatalistic view to be the voice of my False Self: denial. It was a tremendous relief when I first understood that I was creating my own problems, because that meant I could stop creating those problems. By labeling this pattern of victim thinking as the Pleaser, I could get beyond this False Self's way of life. First, however, I had to get out of denial.

*I had not expected what I found. When I finally looked into his eyes during our meeting, I realized that he was initiating a sexual encounter with me after he had known me for ten minutes. I responded to his kisses and his flattery by kissing him back. I responded to his touch by touching him back. I responded to his maleness and strength with a female, passive permission to proceed. Once I acquiesced, I realized my mistake. His touch was rough, his voice was raspy, and his kisses were wet and cold.*

*I knew that I couldn't be what he wanted me to be, but I couldn't find my voice to scream, "Stop!" The voice I had needed to differentiate myself from authorities had never been developed. The voice that had asked questions about the Bible in Sunday school class had never spoken aloud. The voice in the schoolroom that disagreed with or questioned a teacher's opinion had been ignored and stifled. The voice that said "no" to my controlling husband screamed only inside my own head. Its rage echoed out into the darkness of my soul. Where was my voice?*

In the days, weeks and months after the incident with the minister, I asked myself over and over again: Why did I freeze and then run out of his office without standing up for myself? Where was my voice? What was going on inside me that had silenced my truth? I had thought only of pleasing this man and had ignored my own feelings, thus shattering my integrity.

Almost two years passed following the incident with the minister, during which I divorced my husband, I lost my financial security, and lost two business partners. Most importantly, I lost my health.

A recurring infection meant I had to stay home for six weeks for chemotherapy.

On a Sunday morning during this treatment and recovery period, I happened to see the newspaper article. Two young women were filing a lawsuit against the very same minister who had victimized me in his office two years before. I wanted to call them and give them my support, to tell them I had experienced the same inappropriate sexual advances. Eventually, others and I joined the lawsuit.

Before joining the lawsuit, I called my father for his approval. He surprised me by saying in no uncertain terms, "Do not do this. You will get hurt." I guess I had made up my mind before I called him, because I felt terribly hurt that he didn't give me his usual loyal support. In an unusual move toward independence, I felt supporting these women was the right thing to do, even though I knew going against my father's advice was not the Pleaser's style.

But the march toward my own independence came to a halt the moment I met the attorney for the case. My life pattern was to repeat itself one more time before I got it. Since the case was going on just about the time I felt I could make decisions for myself without a man to take care of me, I fell for the comfort of a kindly father figure. His power and charisma seduced me into depending on his advice about what to do and say in the trial. I let him advise me, expecting a large settlement check to take care of my financial problems. I was still thinking that if I got my outside life in order, I would feel better on the inside.

Looking back, I now know it was a way to continue depending on a man to avoid taking responsibility for my life. I was still in denial. Something was missing in my life—I just didn't know it was me. The trial helped me find myself and provided me with another chance to begin to source from within.

*I opened my door for the last client of the day. My client's young child had the TV blaring in the waiting room. The children's program was interrupted by an announcement of the trial's verdict. The jury had found for the plaintiffs, and they had been awarded several million dollars. The exception was Dr. Jayne Gardner. My case had been evaluated separately, and the jury had decided I should be excluded from the settlement.*

*I drove home crying bitter tears. I was mad at everyone, but mostly at myself. Maybe it was time to examine why I was always so willing to please everyone even at the expense of my values.*

At long last, I looked at myself. Through my early morning journaling, I was beginning to figure out what I didn't want to be: a Pleaser. Being a Pleaser was not working for me now. But it was evident that in all my relationships pleasing was the role I normally chose to play. My modus operandi was no longer useful, and I began to think of it as separate from me. I was my own worst enemy. But this part of me was my dark side, my shadow, and I couldn't always see it clearly. I knew the Pleaser was false, but it was dominant. I wondered if there even was a real me.

Everyone has a False Self—that negative, change-resistive part of us who wants to pretend it is all someone else's fault or all our own. Bring your own False Self into awareness by completing Dialogue Two.

---

### **Self-Discovery Dialogue Two**

Defining your False Self's voice

---

*To be nobody—but yourself—in a world which is doing its best, night and day, to make you everybody else—means to fight the hardest battle which any human being can fight, and never stop fighting.*

*ee cummings*

Keep your morning appointment with yourself, continuing to prioritize the first thirty minutes of your day by writing down your thoughts. Your False Self will emerge as your thoughts are put on paper. Your False Self's voice can be identified as a monologue of injunctions that tell you how you should be living, what you need to be doing, and when to worry and doubt. These thoughts are getting in the way of creating the life you want. This is not the essence of who you are, but sometimes we don't know who we are until we know who we are not.

In my writing I began to realize that most of my morning thoughts were about how to please and pacify others. Of course, the pressure brought self-doubt and negativity to the fore.

The next step in hearing your true voice will be to define the voice that has replaced it. The monologue you have been writing is most likely anything but the voice of your True Self.

Reread the last several days of your automatic writing. Next, use a yellow highlighter to color the following thoughts or feelings:

| | |
|---|---|
| Doubts | Negative thoughts |
| Need to's | Worry |
| Regrets | Inadequacy |
| Self-criticism | Perfection |
| Pleasing | Hopelessness |
| Musts & Shoulds | Fears |
| Procrastination | |

Many dialoguers tell me they highlight most of their writing, suggesting the other partner in dialogue, the True Self, is missing. What kind of relationships is the False Self creating for you? What kind of life are these thoughts creating for you? Your True Self will be found in more conscious writing in later dialogues. Right now, we will call all of the negative thoughts listed above your False Self's thoughts.

My journal entry at this stage is still a monologue by the False Self, my Pleaser:

### Author's Journaling for Dialogue Two

*I am so worried today about testifying in the trial. I feel tense and nervous. What will people think of me when they realize I allowed him to touch me without*

> *protest? I am scared they will not respect me as a professional anymore. I know I am upsetting and displeasing my parents with the publicity surrounding this trial. I am terrified because I can't stretch the truth in order to make everyone happy anymore.*

As you can see, my False Self is evident in this writing.

The first time I experienced a client's False Self was with Drew. One day during an office session, I began to have the strangest feeling. I felt the presence of someone else in the room. I tried to ignore it, but it made its presence known, projecting a cold, distant feeling to me. Being very much distracted, I finally mentioned this to Drew. I will never forget the look on his face, both relief and horror that I had discovered this False Self he so badly wanted to hide. I told him I needed to meet his False Self and he reluctantly agreed. Drew slowly stood up from where he was sitting and moved to sit in a chair behind me to the left. I began asking questions of Drew as if he were his False Self. I asked if he controlled Drew's life and he answered yes. This False Self admitted he was tired of protecting Drew from his feelings, which he had been doing since Drew's father had died when he was six years old. Drew was now over fifty. I told his False Self that Drew did not like the way he was being protected from his feelings. The False Self no longer needed to be in control of Drew. His False Self eventually lost its grip on Drew because Drew agreed to let it be recognized and identified.

I'd like to ask you to further delineate your False Self's voice by deciding if there is a general theme or tone to your False Self's writing. Choose one of the following negative themes which best describes your False Self's personality. The theme will most likely be the dominant personality in your automatic writing as well as in your current outside relationships. This part of you has been suppressing and silencing your True Self for years.

| False Self's Personality Style | False Self's Internal Dialogue |
|---|---|
| **Controller** | Get others and the world under control. Clean, organize until controlled. Hard on self and others to "get things under control." |

| Pleaser | Self-doubts abound. Dialogue pushes you to achieve and accomplish. Continually telling self that your ideas and opinions are not as important as those of others. |
|---|---|
| Avoider | Other people will hurt you, so don't trust. Take care of everything yourself. Avoid your feelings. |
| Perfectionist | Control of self. "Never Good Enough" Might try to control such habits as eating, sleeping, etc. Compulsive thoughts. |

| Critic | Blaming of self and others. Negative self-talk. |
|--------|--------------------------------------------------|
| Victim | People should take care of me—poor me. Helplessness. |

From reading my journaling excerpts, you can see that I am always writing about how to please others to the point of betraying myself. This preoccupation was what silenced my true feelings with the minister. Here's an example of a client's writing that shows a self-critical tone, the False Self personality style of Critic:

Bob's Journal Entry

*I am continually making wrong decisions—too*

> *much pressure. I always feel uptight and unable to do*
>
> *my best. Tired. No energy today, Don't want to write*
>
> *because I never can get it right. What does she want*
>
> *me to say? She needs to read my writing and see if it is*
>
> *right or not. Maybe I can never succeed at this*
>
> *dialoguing. My True Self may not be in there.*

Based on the theme of your automatic writing, give your False Self a name. Although I call mine the Pleaser, you can be creative or use the more general terms noted in the chart. Clients have chosen names like Mary Poppins, Never Good Enough, Silencer, and Whiner. The name you choose should indicate how your False Self dominates your thoughts. Don't worry if the right name does not come to you quickly. Your False Self will be working hard to convince you not to define it. After all, if you name it, your True Self might emerge and become stronger than it is!

Give yourself two to three days and then write a name for your False Self here:

---

**Before progressing, settle on one name, even if you are not quite sure of it.**

Spend the next few days allowing your False Self to write for the entire thirty minutes. Regard it from a distance, observing without judgment. This allows your True Self to emerge as the observer; moreover, you might begin to hear the inner dialogue between your False Self and your True Self that has been going on for years. At least for now, you can begin to hear the dominance of your False Self's voice. Stay open to the idea that you can eventually access your True Self's voice.

RESISTANCE: Expect to have negative thoughts about this process. These thoughts are your False Self's voice. Your False Self is a *status quo* keeper and might fight to maintain its stability even though doing so hides your authenticity in the long run. Expect it to try to sabotage this process.

My clients report that the False Self's comments at this point are: "I can't tell if I have a False Self or not." "It is too difficult to define all these thoughts with one theme and name." "I don't think this dialoguing process will work for me." Call on your True Self's native strength and continue. Don't stop writing to yield to your False Self. The more specific you get in identifying this part of yourself, the more power and inner authority will be restored. For example, as I became aware of the Pleaser and could identify its specific thoughts in my writing, I became more conscious of my feelings and learned to make better choices. Through this same process you will begin to distinguish False Self thoughts and True Self thoughts in your writing. This awareness is a threat to your False Self's control. You are now getting out of the False Self's grip and viewing this part of yourself from a distance. Stop to listen to your False Self right now and write down its negative thoughts about this dialogue:

_____

_____

_____

INSIDE WINS: What have you learned about yourself in this dialogue? A win could be just the awareness of the difference between False Self and True Self in your writing.

1.

2.

3.

OUTSIDE WINS: What have you noticed changing in others as a result of your self-discovery work?

1.

2.

3.

CHECKPOINT: Before proceeding to Dialogue Three, make sure you have a clear understanding of your False Self, have selected a name for it, and can identify your False Self's tone of voice in your morning writing.

# Chapter Three:

# Protecting Myself

---

*Past emotional events have shattered the True Self, creating a belief system and personality—the False Self—to protect us.*

---

*For me to be a saint means to be myself. Therefore, the problem of sanctity and salvation is in fact the problem of finding out who I am and discovering my True Self.*

*One's actual self may be far from "real" since it may be profoundly alienated from one's own deep spiritual identity. To reach one's real self, one must in fact be delivered from that illusory and False Self whom we have created ... To use a figure of speech, we must "return to ourselves."*

*Thomas Merton*

Circumstances of birth mark our self-image before we even see the light of day. Being born a girl implied a belief system for me. While born equal, I was taught to feel inferior to boys, and society certainly encouraged that belief. I knew they didn't let girls be ministers. Only the Father, the Son, and the Holy Ghost were mentioned in the prayers at church.

*My straight boyish haircut was perfect for playing outside in the hot Texas summer. No girl clothes for me. I wanted jeans and T-shirts, like all the neighborhood kids. There weren't many kids in the neighborhood, and most of them were boys—my* brother's friends. I wanted to belong to their club, but I wasn't given the password because I was a girl. I tried hard to fit in, but I couldn't spit, hit, kick, or wear my gun and holster strap quite like them. I wanted to be a boy so badly.

In the summer, after chores and vitamins, we would bound through the screen door and head for the vacant lot behind our house. No dance lessons, remedial courses, or soccer camps for us in the summer. Other than having to go to Bible School the first week of vacation, we were free to run wild in the vacant lot. We looked for arrowheads and played out the Western scenes we had seen on our new color T.V. sets.

My chance for acceptance into the boys' private club came one summer when we all decided to build a *fort from the old lumber left by the molding mill in our small town. We knew Mr. Patterson would let us have it, and he did. All we had to do was haul it from his store to the vacant lot and scrape up enough money for nails. We could always use my daddy's tools neatly shelved in the garage.*

*The boys wanted me to draw up the plans for how to build it. They would do the hard stuff, nailing all those boards together. I might get hurt, they told me, but I could help them haul the lumber up the hill and across the city park to the vacant lot behind our house. The hauling took several weeks, but I didn't care that I was only invited to do the grunt work. I so passionately wanted to be a part of them, spitting, kicking, sweating and all.*

*Basically, the older boys bossed the younger ones and me around, a natural hierarchy. As the only girl, I was the lowest "man" on the totem pole. I never questioned the place I was assigned and did what I was told so they would like me.*

*Towards the end of the summer, the fort was finished. We painted it and even built a window to sell lemonade if the club needed to make money. The boys made a sign and posted it on the front of the clubhouse: No Girls Allowed. I had never been part of them.*

*My daddy said later after the tears had subsided that the boys hadn't meant to exclude me. I didn't believe him and knew my daddy made them add: Except Jayne. They grumbled, kicked, and spit when they did it. I knew they didn't really want me in their clubhouse. I felt crushed and hopeless about ever being accepted.*

Remembering my desperate desire to be a boy during those early years brought more clarity to the incident with the minister. I learned that men had more power. I watched my mother ironing, washing, and cooking. I saw my father leaving every day with a briefcase. In my young mind, the father role looked a lot more important. I naturally felt one down to men in general. Add in the title of minister and I felt another notch down the hierarchy.

It took the disappointment of this lawsuit for me to begin to understand a basic spiritual truth: the source of power is within, not without. The ordeal of the trial of the minister helped me to realize the necessity of focusing within more purposefully. The trial generated important shifts for me that took me from a life focused on the external world as my guide and into a life of internal guidance. It marked the beginning of gradually letting go of victimization and embracing of a powerful and productive relationship with myself.

I devised my own ideas of what my False Self, the Pleaser, had done to me. Since my True Self was not running my life at the time, I decided my next step was an examination of how the False Self grew to so dominate my life. It was important to understand the False Self's belief system and what useful functions my False Self performed.

The jury decided that I should have known better. This lesson was the most difficult I've ever experienced. I had spent my whole life striving to please others, to make good grades, to obey authority, and to be respected professionally. Now, my worst fear had been manifested: "People (the jury) declared I was inadequate and not worthy."

Why did I feel so unworthy and shameful based on the results of this trial? Because I had inherited a belief system that said that worthiness depends on the approval of others. It didn't feel like others were approving of me.

Historically, I had been programmed to be a Pleaser. I traced my False Self's origins to my childhood. Its development was the result of being brought up in a world focused on the external. My parents, my school, my church, and my country all conspired against the development of my True Self. I decided to review my early years in an attempt to determine where I'd lost myself. I was to learn that my True Self had been stolen by well-meaning society's expectations.

My father wanted to protect me from war, from the hardships of living on a farm, and from the poverty he'd experienced as a child. He and my mother built a world full of opportunity for me. It was given to me without much effort on my part. They were busy building the world they wished they could have lived in and graciously offered it to my brothers and me. Sacrifice was understood but never mentioned. Here's where I began to see the origins of my False Self, the Pleaser. I should be "pleased" and grateful about this sacrifice.

I remember little about myself in the years before school started. My mother remembers the days before the Pleaser and relates to me that around the age of three I was a serial tantrum-thrower and not afraid of displeasing anyone. She remembers these outbursts occurred regularly on Sundays, when I didn't want to wear a dress to church. In those early years, I had a clear awareness of my feelings and wasn't afraid to be myself even if it wasn't pleasing. I could have, however used some coaching on expressing anger appropriately. I eventually learned that anger was displeasing and lost touch with it. My temper set a healthy boundary: don't make me be something I am not. Anger was proof my True Self was alive and well before I became a quite self-controlled young girl.

My temper tantrums ended by age five or six. After that, I don't remember being mad at anyone anymore. I had already created a strong and ever present False Self, a little personal mask that I wore to please everyone, to fool myself, and to avoid unpleasant feelings. Maybe I had figured out to be loved, you must be pleasing to others. At some point, I began to be very aware of what other people will think.

A false front of pleasing everyone paid off for me in many ways, so I naturally adopted it as a modus operandi. It won me many academic honors. One of these honors put me in a predicament, however. In the fifth grade, I won a declamation award for a poem I recited in class about a little boy in a wheelchair. I remember I liked acting out the part of the little boy and let go of my usual self-consciousness that day even in front of my class members. Looking back, my True Self was present at that moment. But she disappeared on the day I was asked to repeat the performance in front of teachers, parents, and community. The teacher said I had such a natural ease in front of the class she had chosen me to give the poem at a PTA meeting.

I remember stepping out on the school stage. The American flag was on one side, the Texas flag on the other, and a sea of faces was in front of me. They expected a repeat performance. I froze. I remember standing there for hours, but my mother says it was only a few minutes before my teacher came on stage and led me off in humiliation. My False Self had kidnapped the budding little actress with pressure and expectations of perfection.

I never questioned my parents' authority. I fell in line as an obedient child and worked hard at pleasing the parents who worked so hard so I would be happy. I was focused on gaining my parents' approval, even though I still wanted to be a boy and hated wearing dresses.

By the time grade school turned into high school, my True Self was long gone and my False Self prevailed. By seventh grade, I had given up being a tomboy as well as wanting to be a scientist or an artist. Instead, I decided to design my own clothes to create a flawless image and to give looks my highest priority. My best friend tells me she remembers that I announced to her in seventh grade that I wasn't going to make straight 'As' anymore because boys didn't like that kind of girl. Of course, I did not realize at the time that my life was becoming false. After all, everyone else was doing it, and I was rewarded with a great image. Maintaining this image kept me busy and focused on the external world for many years. My inner life was nowhere to be found.

Although my church was a big part of my life, I learned nothing about developing an inner spiritual life. I accepted the church's philosophy without question. Although I often wondered about God, I merely listened to the Sunday school teacher's Bible stories and description of God and Jesus without asking questions. I had many questions, I just didn't ask them. I attended church regularly, where I memorized Bible stories and learned right from wrong but not how to develop a relationship with God or myself.

I was taught that God was outside of me. God was a white-bearded man up in heaven, which was a long way from me. God was a father who would protect me or punish me, as he saw fit. With God so high above me, everything about me seemed less than good enough in the eyes of my church. I did not consider my creative and speculative thoughts about the nature of God important. My thoughts were certainly not in the same league as the church's teachings. Like many of my friends, I fell victim to external control, largely due to how I interpreted the Fifth Commandment, "Honor your father and mother that you may be long upon the land." Thankfully, my parents were honorable people; however, it added to the message not to think for myself. There seemed to be no difference between respect and obedience in my developing belief system.

It became clear from my journal writing that my False Self had integrated messages and beliefs from everyone—my parents, my teachers, and my church.

But I wasn't sure the beliefs of the False Self were really mine anymore. Maybe another part of me in there wanted to determine those beliefs. Maybe I had discovered a new part of me—the True Me.

To help locate your True Self, continue defining your False Self and how it originated to discover how it controls and mutes your True Self.

---

### **Self- Discovery Dialogue Three**

Remembering how your True Self was silenced

---

*Our pathology is our opportunity.*

*Marilyn Ferguson*

In Dialogue Three, you will dialogue directly with your False Self, requesting information from the past about how it originated and what specific beliefs it adopted. The False Self was created to appease the authority figures in your life and protect you from rejection. Some common False beliefs are:

---

### Common False Beliefs

1. There is not enough money, love, energy, or time.

2. I am inadequate and/or powerless.

3. I fear success or failure.

4. I am not worthy.

5. I am afraid to let go and trust.

6. Don't get too happy or something bad will happen.

---

In your morning writing, answer the following questions:

1. What negative message from your family did you receive about yourself that might have helped create your False Self belief system?

   _____

   _____

   _____

   _____

2. What messages about yourself did you get from each parent?

   _____

   _____

   _____

   _____

3.  What beliefs did you develop about men, women, love, and family?

    _____

    _____

    _____

    _____

4.  What beliefs did you form about God?

    _____

    _____

    _____

    _____

5.  What beliefs did you form about money?

    _____

    _____

    _____

    _____

6.  What is the useful function of your False Self?

_____

_____

_____

_____

These messages should fit with the personality type you chose in Dialogue Two. Your False Self learned to protect and hide your authenticity by getting your needs met in one of the following dysfunctional ways:

| | |
|---|---|
| Controlling others or situations | The Controller |
| Being a perfectionist | The Perfectionist |
| Being too pleasing | The Pleaser |
| Feeling you are a victim | The Victim |
| Avoiding your feelings | The Avoider |
| Being critical of yourself | The Critic |

Personality Types based on your False Belief System

Now write down the beliefs you formed about yourself, others, and the world based on the messages you received as a child. Define at least ten False Self beliefs:

1. _____

2. _____

3. _____

4. _____

5. _____

6. _____

7. _____

8. _____

9. _____

10. _____

## Author's False Self-Belief System

1. *Change your true nature to accommodate and please others.*

2. *Be quiet and don't talk about your negative feelings.*

3. *Don't disagree with anyone you want to love you.*

4. *Money is the best way to gain respect from others.*

5. *Girls are not as strong or as capable as boys.*

6. *I must be taken care of by others.*

7. *Spending time on yourself is selfish and bad.*

8. *Always put other people's feelings before your own.*

9. *Your self worth is determined by the outside world's approval.*

---

10. *Men are chosen to be ministers, priests, and preachers and are closer to God than women.*

---

Once I had uncovered my basic belief system, I could fully understand why I hadn't protested the minister's advances.

Here is how former client Dawn identified her False Self. She knew a False Self had controlled her "insides" for as long as she could remember. This False Self had a pattern of put-downs and negative comments she had heard all her life from her family. They had been intent on pushing her to be better at everything. She never felt she measured up. She remembered one attempt by her mother to compliment her: "Dawn, you have the most beautiful face. Your bone structure and complexion are beautiful, but your

hips are too big." Of course, all she could remember
was that her hips were not acceptable to her mother
and thus not to her either.

## Dawn's False Self Beliefs

*It's always your fault.*

*You are not deserving.*

*You are ugly.*

*Don't think you are more than you are.*

*Any happiness is temporary.*

*No matter what happens, never forget you have a problem.*

*Since you are not perfect, you need always to try to improve yourself.*

*Truth is, you will probably never measure up.*

As you see, a theme emerges of oppression and negative thinking. Like most people who were oppressed as children, Dawn heard every comment made to her magnified. She cried when she reread the list, never realizing how severe her False Self's talk was. Her False Self's personality style was Perfectionism. She decided on the name "Never Measure Up" to describe her False Self. This False Self had victimized her all her life. Recognizing her False Self's critical nature released her from the need to criticize other people. Know that you can change these imprints by giving the False Self (your unconscious mind) new beliefs and assumptions with which to operate. Thus the gap between living in your False Self and your True Self begins to close.

<u>RESISTANCE:</u> Your False Self may be threatened by this identification process and attempt to maintain its' dominance.    Here is a letter from a client describing this phenomenon.

Dr. Gardner,

I hope you don't mind me writing you, but I just discovered something.  This morning we touched on getting Mr. Negative under control and I was excited about that.  I got to work and everything was going well, then it hit.  I got upset over something and Mr. Negative went out of control.  It was unbelievable.  I was ready to quit and go home.  I was so out of control!  I started asking myself what was making me so mad.  Then it dawned on me, it's getting rid of Mr.

Negative! Once I discovered this he quieted down. I'm totally blown away by the power of this shift!!!

<u>INSIDE WINS:</u> What three things did you learn about your False Self in this dialogue?

1.

2.

3.

<u>OUTSIDE WINS:</u> How is the new awareness impacting your outside relationships? How are you changing others?

1.

2.

3.

<u>CHECKPOINT:</u> You will have concluded Dialogue 3 when you have determined your top ten false beliefs and feel you are more aware of your False Self's voice.

*How to Change Other People: The Self Discovery Solution*

# Part II:

# Recognizing the Difference

# Between the False Self and the

# True Self

Chapters 4, 5 & 6

## Chapter Four:

## Identifying Myself

*Awareness of the difference in how the False Self and the True Self get our needs met is key to finding the True Self.*

*The outward freedom that we shall attain will only be in exact proportion to the inward freedom to which we may have grown at a given moment. And if this is a correct view of freedom, our chief energy must be concentrated on achieving reform from within.*

*Mohandas Gandhi*

My need for approval began early in life. My False Self got this need met early on by telling me to work hard at pleasing others. In the following memory, my Pleaser saw that my need for love and acceptance was met by focusing on gaining the approval of others and not spending time on the development of my True Self.

*I had overheard my mom tell my daddy to help me learn to ride my bike. My daddy was very busy, and I was glad he had some time for me.*

*I climbed on my bike with no training wheels. My knuckles turned white as I gripped the handlebars. I was scared. Everything was moving too fast inside me. I could see my skinny legs and my knees coming up to almost touch the handlebars as I pedaled. My red Keds were going in circles but kept slipping off the pedals.*

*My daddy was still holding the bike. I was trying hard to do just what he said to do.*

*"Too high," my daddy said. "The seat's too high for a girl, I'll fix it."*

*I wanted to stretch my legs out to look longer to let him know I could reach the pedals just fine with my girl legs. I wished I had my brother's legs.*

*We tried again with my daddy racing along beside me. But every time he let go, the bike wobbled to its side and he was forced to grab the bike and me. My throat was too dry and my head too hot to make a go of it. The side street next to my house was not paved, and Daddy said it was too rough for a little girl and would scrap my knees if I fell. My throat got drier as I remembered my brother riding his bike on that street without worrying about falling. I was scared. I might not ever be able to ride like my daddy wanted me to.*

*My legs didn't wait for my throat to say stop. My daddy's strong brown hands clapped down over my white knuckles and my Keds stayed on the pedals this time. The air raced around me. I knew my daddy wanted me to pedal. I was trying to do what he wanted.*

*I was pedaling too fast for my daddy's legs to stay beside my green and purple bike. I looked back to see how far away he was. The sky moved, and my bicycle looked crooked against it.*

*I could almost feel the scrapes on my knees, but then the brown hands covered mine and the street was under me again where it was supposed to be. My daddy had saved me, but I knew I had goofed up again.*

*He said we would try again tomorrow. I was sad I hadn't been able to pedal better and I was not ready to go in the house. I wanted him to know I could ride like a boy.*

*I felt warm inside, though, when he picked me up and carried me like he used to when I was a baby. My legs wrapped around his waist and I felt very safe and far from the ground as I watched the green grass go by. I wanted to stop him and tell him I'd try harder tomorrow, but my voice wouldn't work.*

*He sat me on the porch and told me to go in and wash up for dinner. I saw him go back and push my green and purple bike toward the garage. I knew I would try harder and harder to please my daddy like my brothers did.*

Many problems in my life were based on the ineffective way my Pleaser had attempted to meet my need for approval. My False Self had been in charge when I thought the minister could give me a spiritual life. My Pleaser wanted everyone to take care of me like my father had done when I was a child. During the trial, my Pleaser had continued the attempt to meet my needs by getting the legal system to right a wrong done to me. My False Self had tried to get acceptance for me from outside sources.

I had always used money, another external source, to create an image of myself as successful, which would win others' approval. Material success was exterior. My False Self created what looked like material success. I drove a nice car. I lived in a nice house. I wore expensive clothes. The truth was on the inside. My charge cards were up to their limit. My car and house payments were huge, and I had little equity in either. The pressure was extreme when I attempted to pay my bills. It was another wrong-side-out area of my life, like my marriage and career.

I reasoned that I needed to work harder to earn more money to pay bills, so I increased my work to 12-14 hour days and some Saturdays. I was now single and supporting two daughters, one in high school and one in college. I felt my career was the one thing I was successful in, so I put more time and energy into working. After all, I had decided early in my life that money was the best way to gain respect and approval from others.

My False Self won approval for me by pushing me to make more money to spend on looking good. Society looked at working long hours as noble. A better way to get that need met would have been to save some of that hard-earned money to take care of my future and peace of mind.

Looking back, I can clearly see my addictive nature at work. I was over-spending, which is an addiction. I was over-working, which is an addiction. I was still not taking adequate care of myself. Most significantly, I was not yet aware of my feelings and needs. The only way I knew to meet my needs was through pleasing people so they would take care of me.

Gradually, my morning writing was becoming more important to me. It was helping me figure things out. I began to identify my needs. Remembering that little girl who wanted more time with Daddy, I knew I mostly needed to be accepted just as I was without doing anything. I knew I needed better self-care, stronger boundaries with people, and the ability to accept and love myself unconditionally. The Pleaser had been busy trying to get others to meet these needs for me. Now I realized I had to find a better way, as others didn't seem to be able to do that anymore.

For me, a big step towards finding my True Self was the realization that I must take care of myself financially, physically, emotionally, and spiritually. Even more important was understanding that I was capable of taking care of myself.

To walk the talk! Now it was time to put into practice some concrete positive changes. It was time to change to a new way of thinking, to develop some new habits in my daily routine that would help me get in touch with who I was, not who others wanted me to be. To find myself, I had to start listening to my inner voice expressing my needs and feelings and to understand my needs. I had to take responsibility to meet those needs in a healthier way. This shift came when I realized that blaming my parents, the minister, and the court system was doing me no good at all. Blame was keeping me stuck. I had to take responsibility for figuring out who I was and who I wanted to be.

I set up a daily plan to meet my needs. Self-care became my top priority. I cut back on my work hours, which resulted in me getting more rest. I also ate more sensibly, which meant I felt healthier. To carry out this plan, I had to challenge another childhood belief: spending time on yourself is selfish.

The second basic need I addressed was boundaries. These were necessary to create enough time in my life to develop a relationship with myself. With strong boundaries, the outside would have less authority. Instead of trying to meet my needs by pleasing others, I learned to protect and care for myself. This was difficult to do because I had always believed I should never disagree with anyone I wanted to love me. Now I rethought that belief. When the minister touched me, I needed to set a boundary that should have been drawn at his first suggestion of discussing my personal sexual life so soon. My False Self's idea that pleasing people would protect me from getting hurt was no longer going to work. I would have to learn to say no. I was turning up the volume on my inner voice—the same voice that had warned me in the minister's office. If someone's words hurt me, I had to express my feelings and set a boundary. If someone touched me inappropriately, a boundary was necessary.

In the incident with the minister, I had felt like a young child of five, innocent and unable to protect myself against a stronger, male adult. But a grown woman would have preferred meeting someone later in the morning. A grown woman would have sat across the room from the minister instead of on the same sofa. A grown woman would not have been looking for approval through a stranger's touch, no matter how much authority he had. A grown woman would be meeting her own needs in a conscious way. This incident would probably not have happened to a grown woman, but if it had, she would have voiced her disapproval at his first touch and reported it the same day, not two years later.

I realized how much I had tolerated the outside world's pressure on me to please instead of setting boundaries that would allow space for my True Self to emerge. My False Self had taken care of my True Self for all those years, pretending to protect her by creating an impeccable outside image. The Pleaser had captured my True Self; my soul had been brainwashed by its captor. I had never known what happened to me.

I began to understand the negative consequences of meeting my needs through pleasing others. I had lost my identity by not learning to set boundaries. My childhood had been spent trying to please instead of trying out my own voice and opinions. I had developed distractions and addictions in an effort to avoid my own feelings for fear others might not accept them. This pleasing style had to go. If I ever wanted to be truly fulfilled, I had to find a new way to meet my needs.

This dialogue will be a discussion between your False Self and your True Self on how to best fulfill your needs.

---

### **Self-Discovery Dialogue Four**

Meeting your True Self's needs

---

*When you can do kindly things to yourself, then you know what it is to be able to love yourself. Then you can look at others who desperately need kindness and love and feel good about their getting it.*

*Gary Zukav*

As you are realizing, most of your automatic writing in the early morning is your False Self's voice talking to you. In this dialogue, you will begin to answer your False Self with your emerging True Self's voice. Identifying and understanding your False Self's voice gives you the awareness that this is not you and that you can formulate new, conscious thoughts.

You must fulfill your needs in healthy ways in order for you to have access to your True Self. If we are not aware of our needs or do not meet them in healthy ways, the False Self attempts to satisfy them. The False Self's activities are typically dysfunctional and are termed "addictions" in modern psychology. They are merely the coping mechanisms of the False Self at work, which is doing what it has always done: protected us from our feelings and from pain we really need to feel in order to heal.

We start with identifying the needs you had as a child—the needs your False Self was created to fulfill. Decide on the one most fundamental need you have right now.

Acceptance

Nurturance

Acknowledgment

Safety

Inner Peace

Unconditional Love

Recognition

Approval

Self-awareness

Self-worth

How did your False Self decide to fulfill this need? Your answer will relate to your False Self's personality. For example, my primary need is approval, so I created a Pleaser personality to get this need met.

Yet filling needs from the perspective of a False Self is less than fulfilling. My Pleaser was working hard at trying to satisfy my need for approval, but no matter how much I achieved, it was never enough. Here's a dialogue I conducted between my False Self and my True Self:

## Author's Dialogue

*False Self: I've been meeting this need for approval for years by trying to please people. I feel they will recognize and approve of me if I always do and say what I think they will like.*

*True Self: And look at the mess with the minister that you got us into by always trying to please people. I was quiet and didn't say anything because you've been in charge so long. I haven't had the chance to express myself.*

*False Self: And how would you have handled the situation?*

*True Self: I would have set more boundaries and taken care of myself better. I need to be more aware of my feelings and be true to myself.*

*False Self:* I just need approval and recognition. Maybe a Ph.D. will help or a best-selling book...

*True Self:* Yes, I'd like that too, but all those accomplishments haven't brought us peace. Maybe we need to satisfy that need in a different way.

*False Self:* How?

*True Self:* We can approve and recognize ourselves instead of looking for outside recognition.

*False Self:* But what would that be like in our everyday life?

*True Self:* Exquisite self-care and daring to conflict with people. Maybe saying no sometimes if you feel they are asking you to do something that

---

*might not be good for you.*

*False Self: But that could displease them.*

*True Self: Yes, that might happen, but maybe, just maybe I might respect myself more for who I am. Then I would feel fulfilled from the inside by living an authentic life.*

---

This demonstrates I was getting my needs met in unhealthy ways, and in the future, that awareness would allow me to start getting my needs met in healthy ways.

Now, allow your False Self to share one example of a mistake you made that was caused by trying to meet a primary need in an unhealthy way.

_____

_____

_____

Then carry on a dialogue between your True Self and your False Self ending with the True Self offering an example of a healthy way to meet that need.

_____

_____

_____

The development of boundaries and the fulfillment of your needs go hand in hand. In order for you to have space to discover your True Self, you must set some boundaries on your outside world. Boundaries protect your well-being and define you as unique. You draw a line around you that permits only acceptable behavior from others. For example, no one may yell at you or touch you sexually without your permission. No one may be critical of you. Boundaries need to be in place to give us the emotional space we need to experience our feelings and become more self-aware. What changes in your life could you make in order to fully meet and satisfy this need?

_____

_____

_____

Jana first appeared at my office having just been released from the hospital. Her concussion and broken ribs were healing. Her broken heart was not healing, however. Her husband had beaten her the night before. Jana had been married for 22 years and had two children. She was a published author, both talented and beautiful, although quite unaware of it. Her True Self was, at the time, unavailable to her. In her home environment Jana experienced no relief from victimization. Her home was just not safe, and when she attempted to do her morning writing her False Self would protect her by shutting her down. She made a decision to set a much-needed boundary, allowing herself a safe place to reconnect with herself. She decided she was strong enough to live on her own until her husband got some help. Once away from him, her False Self could let down the wall of protection that was preventing her from connecting with her True Self.

Jana's story illustrates the need to set good boundaries. It also illustrates that Jana was working on herself, and not trying to change her husband.

Tom, another client, sought my help to change his daughter into a more responsible young adult. I encouraged him to do his own work.

## Tom's Needs

*Tom illustrates someone like me externally pulled by the needs of others. Society had taught him well. The first basic belief we uncovered was: "First be a good husband, father and provider. If there is any time left, you may nurture your own needs."*

*We discovered that by putting his own needs last, he rarely got around to doing anything he personally valued. As we identified his True Self, he confided in me that he once won a gold medal for his singing in a barbershop quartet. Harmonizing with other men's* voices was fun, and he passionately loved his time spent in song.

I handed him a list of needs and asked him to pick out his top need. He chose self-worth. He realized upon identifying this need that he had been living without integrity the last few years, sacrificing his own needs for those of his family. He had felt this sacrifice was justified and would eventually bring the love and respect of others. But as so often happens, the loved ones he was enabling became more demanding of his time and money and less appreciative. As a result, he was empty and discontent, as were they.

Tom realized that he had been focusing his time on others, putting little time into the rejuvenation of his True Self. His False Self, named Mr. Fix-It, dominated *his life.*

*I challenged Tom to satisfy his needs in a healthy, up-front way. He accepted the challenge and found a barbershop quartet. He set some boundaries with his wife and children about his own time. He began to feel more content and fulfilled. The side benefits were that his marriage improved and his daughter found a job and moved into her own apartment.*

RESISTANCE: Clients have more resistance with this dialogue than any other. Denial is based on the belief that someone will someday take care of us and we won't have to do it ourselves. As you know by now, that is False Self talk. The True Self knows it is better to meet your own needs or ask up front for help from others.

INSIDE WINS: Name three successful ways you are learning to meet your needs.

1.

2.

3.

OUTSIDE WINS: List three ways you are changing other people because of your self-discovery.

1.

2.

3.

CHECKPOINT: Knowing what your top need is, and accepting responsibility to get that need met in a healthy way.

## Chapter Five:

## Growing Myself Up

---

*The False Self helps us avoid our feelings;*

*The True Self is our feelings.*

---

*If you want to know what's true for you about something, look to how you are feeling about it. Feelings are sometimes difficult to discover—and often even more difficult to acknowledge. Yet hidden in your deepest feelings is your highest truth.*

*Neale Donald Walsch*

By taking responsibility for meeting some of my own needs, I respected myself more. Perhaps that action pushed back a curtain; I could acknowledge my feelings and see the real me.

*It was the favorite photograph of the family, nicely framed and still hanging in my mother's picture gallery in the hall outside their bedroom. One visit, I stopped to look more closely at this early picture.*

*In the picture, I am around eight years old. My parents, my two brothers, and I are standing outside our little gray and white house in our Easter clothes. We are all holding Bibles. My mother's linen suit is decorated with a white and pink lily, and I am carrying an arm corsage and wearing white gloves. I am wearing black patent Mary Janes and white socks with ruffles, a petticoat, a lavender cotton dress with lace and an Easter Bonnet which covered up my Toni curls—all the stuff I really hated. At one point in my* life, I would have been absolutely repulsed at the mere sight of the Easter outfit I was so proudly wearing.

I looked at the photo again and realized I had nothing to fear. My True Self <u>was</u> alive and well after all. My little cherub face was glowing because, bless my pure little heart, I was sticking my tongue out. It was subtle—not mean but a quiet statement to the world that I knew what they were doing to me and it tasted bad. My True Self was still present somewhere at that time in my life. The lavender, the gloves, and the curls couldn't hide the real me. With relief, I knew that history held the secret to who I was.

Suddenly I got it. No. I should say my body received the message first. Deep within, I was reacting to the picture with a primitive eruption of truth. They thought they had pulled it off. Old, stored-up rage and *anger flooded me as the reality of how I had been raised came to my consciousness by way of my body. My body felt hot and restless. I had been captured and rewired. I had allowed them to kidnap me. My False Self had shoved that tongue back in my mouth at some point, using shame to gag me.*

*I was furious and knew I must honor the anger that was finally erupting in me. I raced to get my journal and poured out my outrage, censoring nothing: Fooled. Tricked. Murdered. Muffled. Cajoled. Shamed. Molded. Shaped. Killed. Deprived. Hushed. Muted. Overthrown. Tackled. Blanketed. Stopped. Overridden. Quieted. Changed. Coerced. Handled. Smothered. Sliced. Maimed. Hollowed out. Emptied. Replaced. Overturned. Rewired. Reprogrammed.*

*The words came tumbling out of my being. They were me. I owned these unacceptable feelings the words represented with pride. I loved the anger pouring out of me. I knew it was my original score, music I had written. No one else would ever react as I had. These were my feelings, and I was deeply proud of them. They represented the real me. Who I was came dancing out into the light.*

*My False Self started screaming at me to stop. Don't go there, she said. You will regret it. You will be hurt. People won't like this. Your parents are kind, loving people and will be hurt by this revelation. Your church was just trying to help you grow up to be a lovely, sweet woman. Your teachers felt their job was to tell you what was right and wrong. The old, internal patriarch had been waiting for the next fresh feeling to*

115

*surface. It would take that feeling and bury it deeply in those old hidden places.*

*But it was too late for the Pleaser to push me back into the blackness and numbness of denial. I was out, and the secret was blown. I had found myself, and the reunion was sweet. No one could retract the truth I felt in my bones. I knew I must protect my future feelings from being killed off by honoring my present ones.*

*I wrote and wrote and wrote until the heat had cooled before I dared to share my feelings with anyone who might unknowingly reason me out of myself again. As a result, life came back to me.*

Denying my own feelings had made my life as a child solitary. I remember feeling intensely lonely, longing for my father's time and my mother's touch. I wanted my daddy to spend more time with me—a girl.

I cling to the few memories of times when he did— when he helped me learn to ride my bicycle or when he carried me in his arms to the doctor's office after my tonsillectomy. He is such a loving man. I regretted not seeing him more. I felt he was disappointed in me, and I remember trying harder to get his approval. I didn't want to be a princess because society said men were more important than women. I wanted my daddy to want me to go to work with him like my brothers. I wanted to carry a briefcase, not stand at an ironing board all day. I wanted him to think I was smart and could be a boss of a business someday, like he was. It was easier, however, to just be dependent on him and let him take care of me, which he did very well.

I wanted my mother's hands to touch me more. I remembered her hands when she played the piano and when we washed dishes and ironed together. I remembered what those hands looked like when she smoothed the bed linens as she made up the beds every morning. I could see those hands molding Valentine candy and hanging washing on the line. I wanted her hands to touch my face and pick me up and hold me. I remember thinking if I silenced myself and turned my real voice down maybe I would get more of her loving touch. Instead, I settled for her thoughts. She was always thinking about what the neighbors thought, so I did too. I knew she wanted me to do well at school and behave for the teachers and be caring and sweet to my friends. I tried hard to do what would please her.

I hurt for the loss of the high-spirited child I was originally. I felt sad for the little schoolgirl trying so hard to always get As to please the teachers. I got angry remembering being nine years old and visiting my cousin's church. I was pressured to walk down the aisle "to be saved," although I had already been saved at my own church. I was angry that no one answered my questions in Sunday school about where Cain's wife came from or why God was a man and only had a son.

I longed to be myself again—to understand, know, and love who I was. In order to create space for my true self to emerge, I needed to clean out my emotional closet of all the old anger and resentment that had been packed up in boxes over the years. I longed for joy in my life, even if it meant facing and accepting my anger.

The True Self's voice will emerge in dialoguing as you become more aware of your own feelings.

---

### <u>Self-Discovery Dialogue Five</u>

Locating Your True Self

---

*Be the change you want to see in the world.*

*Mohandas Gandhi*

The only way to positively identify and connect with your True Self is if the discovery process penetrates the heart. Neuroscientists are becoming more convinced the emotional brain (your True Self) is able to override the rational brain (the False Self.) We connect more deeply through our emotions, and if expressed appropriately, they define who we are. The goal of this dialogue is to find your heart. Your False Self's voice in your writing comes without much effort, usually by just copying down your thoughts. To get a feel for your True Self's voice, let's start at the beginning. Try to remember how you felt growing up. Feelings are like messengers of the truth. They tell us what is going on. Anger warns us we are being violated. Fear means a threat. Sorrow means empathy for someone suffering or for you. The only bad emotion is one that has become stuck, so part of developing a positive relationship with yourself means embracing the full spectrum of emotions in your True Self.

Buried feelings never die. They fuel the False Self's dominance and silence the voice of the True Self. They motivate our False Self to protect and isolate us from our present feelings, trapping us in illogical and dysfunctional behaviors. Dialogue with your child-self and answer the following questions using first person. Keep an old photograph of yourself as a child in view. Accept all of the feelings s/he expresses with unconditional acceptance. Don't minimize or downplay any feelings.

1. Describe your feelings at a time in your life when someone treated you unfairly.

_____

_____

_____

_____

2. Describe how you felt as a child in your family.

_____

_____

_____

3. Are there people in your life (child or adult) who have truly hurt you? Name them and briefly describe how they hurt you.

_____

_____

_____

For each example you listed in the three questions above, fill in the following statements.

I am angry because

_____

_____

_____

I am sad because

_____

_____

_____

_____

### Charlotte's Story

*Charlotte was single—and lonely. She came to me for help in finding her soulmate. I challenged her to find herself first. Was she willing to take a three month course in self-discovery? She had been rejected in two prior relationships and wondered if there was something wrong with her, or did she just pick the wrong men. I suggested that perhaps she just needed to learn to love and accept herself before she could expect love from anyone else. She reluctantly agreed and completed the first four dialogues without an issue. When we began to discuss her work on*

*Dialogue Five, I could hear the distress in her voice. She told me she hadn't felt any emotion in years and wanted to learn to feel again. However, she hadn't been prepared for the intensity of the anger that she had felt during this dialogue.*

*When she was five, her mother told her that she was not smart enough to start kindergarten. Her older brothers and sisters had been attending school all of her life, and she had always felt left out. She wondered, at five, if that meant she would never be able to go to school. She felt unacceptable. This false belief forced her to create a False Self, The Unacceptable, to protect her from the resulting feelings. She grew up accepting this as the truth and always considered herself less that others and thus, undesirable. Her False Self's function was to hold back the sadness from her consciousness, to keep her from being overpowered by the feelings. As a result, Charlotte had done poorly in school.*

*Discovering this truth, Charlotte began to feel some justified anger at her mother, and some compassion for herself. "It is not necessary to blame your mother," I told her. "It is necessary to take responsibility for where you are and move forward." I also told her it was healthy to validate her feelings and recognize the resulting consequences on the patterns of behavior in her life and relationships.*

## Luther's Story

*Luther, a seventy-eight year old man, came into my office. He arrived at his family's urging, because he* was depressed and withdrawn. Luther was a veteran of World War II and had been stationed on a submarine in the Pacific along the shores of Japan. He was, like my father, very young—only in his late teens or early twenties—during World War II. During his sessions with me, he wished no analysis; his only need was for a safe place to tell his war stories. He told me about many hardships and about night terrors. He described the time his ship ran short of rations and could not restock due to the war. He and his shipmates saw the supplies dwindling. Meals became a clear broth or a few beans. He watched his friends lose weight and became aware of the pounds he was losing. He wondered if he would live through the war.

He stored up those memories and feelings, never

*divulging them to anyone before. He told me he never cried, while tears ran down his weathered cheeks. It was like gathering information on my father's life as he had been stationed in a foreign country during the same period. I felt I understood more of why my father worked so hard when I was growing up—to hold back his feelings, like Luther.*

*Luther told me once that he knew he had been changed by the trauma of the war. He came home and decided to forget the past. This was a noble goal, but it was difficult to do. He tried to side step those feelings for the rest of his life. Luther seemed to be cleaning out his emotional closet one box at a time to gain enough relief to return to his life without the burden of repressed emotions.*

The above stories illustrate how your False Self blocks your feelings from your consciousness and thus protects you from the reality of life.

<u>RESISTANCE:</u> Your False Self will resist the return of old feelings, as well as compassion for yourself. Stay true to yourself by acknowledging your true feelings without worrying about hurting other people's feelings.

<u>INSIDE WINS:</u> What feelings are returning for you?

1.

2.

3.

<u>OUTSIDE WINS:</u> How are you expressing your feelings differently now in your relationships?

1.

2.

3.

<u>CHECKPOINT:</u> Realizing compassion for yourself, you will be more open to feeling some emotions at this point in the dialogues.

# Chapter Six:

# Forgiving Myself

> *The False Self clings to the past and repeats historical patterns; the True Self learns from the False Self's mistakes, forgives, and moves on.*

*Forgiving won't make the offense all right. It will make you all right.*

*Beth Moore*

My False Self's pleasing pattern began when I believed I had to deny my feelings, my gut, and my intuitions in order to be loved and accepted. The pattern rolled out into personal relationships as repressed, lack of assertiveness, avoidance of conflict, self-doubt, and dependent powerlessness.

*My teacher called my name and congratulated me; I would be the first-grade princess in the school contest for raising money for the P.T.A. She took my hand and slowly walked me into the hall, where Mrs. Velma's and Mrs. Kitchen's classes were filing out into the hall. There were no girls in the hall, only boys.*

*Mrs. Roberts, my teacher, said to pick out a boy to be my prince in the contest. I felt like I shouldn't be the only girl in the hall, and I wanted the boys to still play with me. They were all very quiet, and their faces didn't look the way they did when they were on the playground.*

*I couldn't move, so my teacher took my hand and walked me up and down the dark hall. I could still* smell the chalk dust from where the class monitor had dusted the erasers near the door outside. My saddle shoes moved up and down the hall. I didn't understand the assignment but would try to do it right.

I slowed down near the door to my own schoolroom and just wanted to dash back inside and be like everybody else. "Point," my teacher said. I pointed to a boy I liked to play with on the slide on the playground. "Alan, you will be her prince," the teacher said. I was afraid to look back at Alan, but I heard the other boys snicker before I went back inside my room.

I felt miserable all day. I couldn't wait until the bell rang so I could tell my mother how upset I was at being a princess.

*I raced to the car where my mother was waiting. The teacher was behind me. She told my mother I was elected the class princess and to please sew me a princess dress for the football game.*

*My mother was very happy. We stopped at the dry goods store and bought colored net and pink satin for the dress. She made me a diamond headband to match and curled my hair on pink spongy curlers that made my head feel all tight and scratchy. I hated the rough net of the princess dress. I hated the feeling I had when I saw my boy friends' faces. And Alan, my prince, looked very mad at me.*

*I wanted to rip the dress off and never be a princess again, but I saw that my mother was very happy. I smiled and decided this pink dress would be OK...*

Based on a life-long pattern of satisfying my needs externally and being unaware of my own feelings, I learned to depend on and eventually blame others for how I felt. But the blaming was just one extreme of my dependence. My incredible ability to put other people's feelings before my own blocked the doorway to my True Self. I had always been immobilized by my sympathy for others. Yes, I could hear my mother's voice saying, "This is a good thing, Jayne." But my external focus was an extreme, just like the blaming. It was the cause of the anger and the resentment, in fact. How could I grow up when all I ever thought about was others?

The very idea of focusing on myself still overwhelmed me with guilt. Yet, somewhere inside, I had opened up one too many boxes of repressed guilt, and the real me was getting stronger. I had continued to use the Pleaser mentality repeatedly, expecting a father, a husband, or a minister to take care of me. The Pleaser felt she was not capable of being successful in life on her own.

The definition of this pattern opened my eyes to what had caused the ending of so many hurtful relationships in my life. Now I understood why I had stopped loving my husband. Stuffing my anger at him contributed to the demise of the relationship. I hadn't felt like I could be a businessperson myself and thus had poured my ambition into him. I had lost two business partners because I blamed them for my money problems. I had avoided conflict and doubted myself. I had fired several secretaries because I failed to tell them what I wanted and then was mad when they didn't read my mind. And then, of course, there was the situation with the minister, where I acted out the same lack of assertiveness and self-doubt. Swallowing my anger at the minister's invasion of my privacy had not worked out very well, either.

These unhealthy patterns had resulted in unhealthy relationships. I could feel myself turning the anger I felt at others against myself. I wanted two things to result from this self-discovery: to let go of the anger at others and to find inner peace and self-love that only self-forgiveness could offer.

I had been in an abusive relationship with myself for a long time. The Pleaser had learned to beat me up with my own anger. I was angry with myself for not challenging the messages my parents sent me or my husband and the minister's abuse. To get to the inner peace I wanted, I would have to forgive myself for scrambling for others' approval for the last forty years.

I wanted to release my parents from my anger and myself from my guilt for being angry at them. Upon consideration, my parents had not created my beliefs. I had interpreted their actions to mean they respected money and material success. Upon reflection, they were community servants, giving their time and money back to the town and the church. I could see them more as people and less as parents.

The belief that money brought approval and acceptance was my own. I wanted to rethink what was important to me, not to base it on what I <u>thought</u> my parents believed but to decide what Jayne Gardner valued. I wanted to acknowledge this past, stored-up anger so I could let it go and it could let go of me.

I had the most difficulty with letting go of the anger at myself for filing the lawsuit. Even the jury suggested I should have known better. The minister had used my devotion and my eager-to-please, self-sacrificing personality. Why had I followed up an immature act with another childish attempt to blame the minister? Yes, he had done something wrong; but as an adult, I had chosen to be submissive. Why had I not filed a letter of complaint, testified at the trial for the other women, and not tried to replace the loss of my faith with money? I was mad at myself and at my church.

That was the scariest. Why had my church betrayed me by keeping silent during the trial? I had grown up trusting the church to tell me what was right and wrong. Wasn't what this man had done to all those women, including me, wrong? I knew my church had cowered behind its stained-glass windows.

All that is needed for forgiveness is a willingness to let go of the resentment that had been accumulating over the years. I willingly released the anger through my morning writing, and I hastened the process by conducting a series of workouts, releasing my anger at a punching bag I purchased at the local athletic supply store. This physical release might have been the key that connected the willingness in my mind with the deep-seated feelings in my body and let them go.

Just as soon as I understood and accepted the anger, it was gone. Unacknowledged resentment had blocked me from peace for a long time. I could now feel it dissolving. Most of the anger I had stored up had been at myself. I felt compassion for the woman I was and am—a woman willing to go up against an entire religion for what she believed in. The very understanding and acknowledgement of my own truth freed me from its grip. I could sense my body letting go of the urgency that had driven me for so many years to achieve, accumulate, and accommodate. The forgiveness seemed to heal the part of me that was pushing and driving me to prove I was acceptable.

As I wrote in my journal, I finally felt compassion for my parents, who had only wanted me to be happy. I even felt sorry for the Pleaser, who had tried so hard to let others make me happy. With this feeling of compassion came self-acceptance, approval, and forgiveness. Both my parents and I had been working so hard toward the same goal—to do what was right and ultimately to please God.

I could feel a little more truth seeping into me; maybe God had always loved me, Pleaser and all. Maybe my feelings were acceptable to God, even my anger. Could God be <u>in</u> those feelings? No one else could ever give me what I already had within myself; God was on the inside and the true source of love.

All the negativity I was releasing arose because of the encounter with the minister. I saw the crisis was actually a blessing. My view of the past was now different. I accepted my parents' love for me as I accepted myself. Over time I forgave the minister, my parents, and myself. I was learning and growing from my mistakes. Forgiving myself and others freed me to take responsibility for my own life.

It is necessary to take responsibility for your feelings and forgive yourself and others.

---

**Self-Discovery Dialogue Six**

Taking responsibility for yourself

---

*If we were to abuse our children, Social Services would show up at our doors. If we were to abuse our pets, the Humane Society would come to take them away. But there is no Creativity Patrol or Soul Patrol to intervene if we insist on starving our souls.*

*Clarissa Pinkola Estes*

A True Self assumes responsibility for past feelings and lets go of the accumulated resentment. When your True Self forgives, you no longer have to carry the burden of such negative experiences. You can make room for love, peace, and fulfillment.

It might be a stretch for you to assume responsibility for forgiveness. It does not mean what happened to you was your fault, but continuing to hold on to such negativity is your fault. True forgiveness means you must not hold others responsible for your present experiences. If you do not hold yourself accountable for forgiving, you will continue to be in a negative, blaming, False-Self state of mind. Forgiveness helps you regain the power and voice of your True Self.

If you have been unable to forgive someone, your False Self is holding you back and protecting you from your feelings by burying them. You must call on your

True Self to help you release them. Non-forgiveness and negativity are the opposite of the True Self.

From the list of people who hurt you in your life, now write letters of forgiveness to each person. You will not mail these letters, only use them to resolve the issues in your heart.

_____

_____

_____

_____

Now the hardest task is to forgive yourself for any mistakes you have made in your life. Ask your True Self to list your major regrets in life so far:

_____

_____

_____

_____

Realize that your False Self was just trying to satisfy your needs when you made these mistakes. Allow yourself to feel compassion. I see my False Self as a teacher, so write a letter to your False Self forgiving yourself for these mistakes and regrets.

_____

_____

_____

_____

## Melinda's Forgiveness

*Melinda wanted me to help her make her husband more loving. She said her life was almost picture-*

*perfect. She had three children, a hard-working husband, good friends, and enough money to live comfortably. She came to me because her husband was angry that she could not enjoy sex. In fact, she detested their lovemaking.*

*Going back quickly to examine her emotional closet, she emptied the contents of one heavy box. She had moved to the U.S. from Mexico. Because of abusive parents, she had left home at sixteen, pregnant and husbandless. She had supported herself during the pregnancy and through government assistance made it through the birth of the child and returned to work rather than continue to accept food stamps. Her existence at seventeen was hard and poverty-ridden. Her baby was in daycare all day. She accepted a job out of desperation at a topless bar. She hated the dancing, but the money far exceeded what she could make as a sales clerk at a local department store.*

*One day an older man approached her after one of her dances and offered her a job where she could stay home with her child and even start college. The job was to have sex with him for a couple of hours once a week. He would pay for everything, including getting her a nice apartment and babysitter so she could go to school. He was offering her a ticket out of destitution. She accepted and for two years met the job's requirements.*

*Years later she was married and happy except for sex with her husband. She got nauseated making love to the man she truly loved. Her False Self's chatter was unforgiving and told her bad things about herself. She described all the negative beliefs and declared the False Self's name to be "Greed." She knew she had sold her soul for money.*

*We then detailed her positive strengths regarding her True Self. She was a good parent, a faithful wife, and a strong Christian. She was trying to live a good life. Her primary need was for self-acceptance. She began to focus on her True Self and not her old beliefs, which her False Self had been unconsciously controlling for her.*

*She initiated a dialogue between her False Self, Greed, and her True Self and discovered Greed felt it needed to protect her from having sex again because the sexual aspect of her old job had caused her so much emotional pain. Melinda told Greed she no longer needed to be protected from sex and that it should hang around and protect her from real danger. As she learned to forgive herself, her sexual desires for her husband increased. The changing of the guard brought her back into harmony. She changed herself, and the result was that her husband became more loving.*

## Al's Story

Karen and Al called me for help with their son, Andrew. He was three years old and had been to see other therapists, who had diagnosed oppositional/defiant disorder. The child had shown angry behavior not normal to a three-year-old. Inquiring into their parenting, Al admitted having problems controlling his own anger when disciplining his son. As Al progressed through the program, he remembered himself being mistreated as a child and he still harbored anger at his own father. In his dialoguing Al wrote that Andrew had been unplanned, and that the birth of the baby had forced him to drop out of law school. He had sacrificed a life long dream. His suppressed anger was released on the child at discipline time, far out of proportion to the offense. No wonder they had an angry child on their hands. Once Al worked through his anger he was able to forgive his parents. He was then able to take the emotional charge out of his parenting. Al's inner change released his son from a family pattern of anger and returned Andrew to a normal childhood. An inside win and an outside win.

<u>RESISTANCE:</u> Letting go is hard work. Remember that forgiveness happens inside you. You will witness tremendous changes in your relationships by completing this dialogue. Stay diligent.

<u>INSIDE WINS:</u> What is the result of the forgiveness work you did in this dialogue?

1.

2.

3.

<u>OUTSIDE WINS:</u> How has this forgiveness work impacted your current relationships with loved ones?

1.

2.

3.


<u>CHECKPOINT</u>: Forgiveness is the biggest block to reaching your True Self, so continue to write until you have forgiven others and yourself.

Before moving into Part III, here's a summary of the differences between your False Self and your True Self. The hardest part of dialoguing is to recognize the other voice, your True Self. A distinction develops between your False Self and your True Self. A conscious oriented state is a True Self presence. A robotic, habitual reaction is an unconscious or a false state of mind. Here are some other distinctions that might help.

| True Self State of Mind | False Self State of Mind |
|---|---|
| Imaginative | Resentful |
| Creative | Blaming |
| Present oriented | Negative in thinking |
| Confident | Unaware of feelings |
| Conscious | Zoned out |

| Aware of Feelings | Helpless |
| --- | --- |
| Knows own opinion | Manipulative |
| Focuses on strength, not weakness | Covert |
| Spontaneous | Hidden agenda |
| Playful | Confused |
| Joyful | Addictive |
| Open | Doubtful |

*Jayne Gardner, Ph.D.*

# Part III:

# Developing a Relationship

# Between your False Self and

# your True Self

## Chapters 7, 8, & 9

*Jayne Gardner, Ph.D.*

# Chapter Seven:

# Pumping Up My True Self

---

*The False Self served a useful and protective purpose,*

*but now must serve the True Self.*

---

*No power outside ourselves can bring us what we truly need. Those needs do not perish, do not come and go, and are always reliable.*

*There is only one source of all power, all wisdom, and all Love, and it has its life within us, all around us, and IS us. We are One with it. We can only "protect" temporary needs outside ourselves and watch them manifest only to pass away. If we put our trust into false gods, they will eventually let us down. Be they people, jobs, government, circumstances or any temporary thing. Let us seek Truth in the only source where it exists, within!*

*Josh McIntosh and Rev. JoAnn "Amanda" Polito*

As I focused more and more on my True Self, and the chatter of the Pleaser became not quite so loud, I wanted to act on this living from the inside out. I knew that I was ready to get out of my head and into action. I was to engage in some real spiritual warfare when I put the True Self in charge. I wanted to experience my True Self in action and deliberately staged an outing to test my ability to stay in my True Self.

*A colleague, Chuck, had been insisting that rock climbing would help me build confidence. I asked him to take me out to the cliffs.*

*When I was hitching up my hiking boots the next morning, my stomach was less sure. When I saw the cliffs, I knew I had made a mistake. But I was still too externally directed to pull out and look cowardly. The challenge proved to be just the opportunity my True Self needed to make the shift into empowering my decisions.*

*I chose a point on the side of the rocks that I felt I could attain and made that my goal for the first climb. My heart lurched. I was amazed at my eagerness to begin the climb.*

*During the first steps I heard Chuck's voice, calm and deliberate, walking me through what to do next and where the safe hand- or footholds were. If I missed a grab and slipped, his rope caught me. I still felt the awful fear in that split second before the rope caught*

161

*me, but it always did, and I began to trust the process. I kept climbing higher. Chuck's voice was a comfort. He gradually saw that I could figure out which rocks would work to lift me up, just how to raise my upper body, and when to push or pull. I gained some confidence and developed a rhythm.*

*I did well reaching the next finger-hold until I looked down at Chuck standing below me. I hadn't realized how far up I had climbed. I felt dizzy and unsure of myself, disoriented. I cried to myself, why am I doing this? I yelled at Chuck to get me down as soon as possible.*

*There was a pause. Chuck is a good coach and thus good at pauses. Finally, he said, "Sure, Jayne. You can get down anytime. However, I still think you can make your goal. Why don't you rest for a minute, go inside, and realize how far you've come?"*

*I breathed, went inside, and started up again, edging my way.*

*I had come within five feet of my goal when the footholds disappeared. I could not find a place to put my feet. I searched and brainstormed, bent on finding a solution until I looked down again. I decided to start down but soon realized I could not retrace my steps. Where was a girl's daddy when she really needed him? I was stuck. "What am I going to do now?" I yelled in my panic to Chuck. I wanted him to give me the answer, but from 50 feet below he could barely see the next ridge I was headed for.*

*His voice started up again and the very sound quieted me. He was still there. He said to me the line* we still joke about: "I don't know, Jayne—what are you going to do now?"

I had gotten myself up there; it would be up to me to get back down or go to the top. I felt physically exhausted, sweaty, and my legs were shaking. I closed my eyes and suffered. My False Self was chattering that I was a girl and not capable of getting down by myself. But now I was aware of the Pleaser's antics and messages of self-doubt. Another part of me was observing and wanting to prove the Pleaser wrong.

In rock climbing, there is a step called a "commitment move." This is the moment when you have to let go of solid ground to move to the next higher place. It can be scary. I was facing it now.

Chuck told me I could get to the goal if I still wanted to. "Keep trying," he said.

*Suddenly, I saw a rock I had not noticed before. It had one little ledge jutting out barely enough for me to get my fingers around. If I could reach it, I could get a handhold to pull myself up and see a rock where I could get a foothold for my left foot. I felt myself reach up to the rock. This time there were no screams, only tears. I had done it.*

*A short time later, I learned to rappel and felt the exhilaration of going down after a hard climb up. I congratulated myself and knew it was my True Self in action taking care of me.*

As I spent more time with myself in my morning writing, a sharp inner image began to surface. I no longer wanted the Pleaser to run my life. I knew I wanted my True Self to fill the emptiness. I wanted a clear image of what my True Self was like. I wanted what I had before my parents' expectations, the church's doctrines, and the school's need for obedience took over. I wanted to know what I would have been like if I had been encouraged to develop my imagination and make my own decisions. In short, I wanted to be my original self. I knew that self would be the core of my True Self.

Suddenly, I realized that I was happier and more peaceful than I'd ever been before. I had little money, an older car, an apartment instead of a house, and last year's clothes. But I had plenty, I concluded, more than enough.

Everything that would happen to me in the future would provide me with an opportunity to choose a different way of being—the true way for me. I was beginning to hear my True Self's voice.

In this dialogue, it is time for you to make a shift from the False Self's lead to putting your True Self in charge.

---

### **Self-Discovery Dialogue Seven**

Making the Shift

---

*Growth is the one evidence of life.*

*Cardinal Newman*

To create a positive relationship with yourself, and change your inner dialogue, begin by rewriting your old beliefs. What beliefs will you want to give up to become your True Self? Refer back to Dialogue 3 for your False Self beliefs. Here is how I changed mine.

## Author's False Self Beliefs

1. Your self worth is determined by the outside world's approval.

2. Girls are not as strong and capable as boys.

3. Always put other people's feelings before your own.

4. Change your true nature to accommodate and please others.

## Author's True Self Beliefs

1. I am a worthy and deserving person.

2. I am a strong and capable woman.

3. I am conscious of my own feelings and express them appropriately.

4. I hear the inner voice of my True Self and express my True Self in all my relationships.

**In the same manner, rewrite your False Self beliefs below. Then reframe each of them into a True Self belief. Use present tense. Refer to your list on page 43.**

1.

2.

3.

4.

5.

6.

7.

8.

9.

10.

## Your True Self Beliefs

1.

2.

3.

4.

5.

6.

7.

8.

9.

10.

You are now ready to compose a letter to your False Self, notifying it of a major change in your life.

You will not allow your inner dialogue to be controlled by the False Self. The False Self will still be present in your life, but it will no longer be in charge. This dialogue will symbolize the changing of the guard. Your False Self will begin to serve the development and growth of your True Self. Here are some ideas:

Dear False Self:

1. Thank you for saving my life when I was in danger as a child.

2. Your purpose was to keep me safe.

3. My True Self is now strong enough to take care of me.

4. Your way of protecting me is antiquated and no longer needed.

5. I wish you to tell me when I am in a dangerous place, but distractions and addictions are no longer needed to keep me safe.

6. My True Self is capable of expressing my feelings and seeing that my needs are met responsibly.

7. Your old beliefs no longer run me.

8. I am able to listen to my body and intuition and can manage decision-making.

9. This letter serves as your final notification of a changing of the guards. <u>The official inner authority is now the True Self.</u>

When you are ready, compose your letter below.

Dear False Self:

_____

_____

_____

_____

_____

_____

_____

_____

_____

_____

_____

_____

_____

_____

_____

_____

_____

_____

_____

_____

_____

_____

_____

_____

_____

Brad entered coaching with me because his marriage was suffering; he felt his wife needed to make some changes. He accepted the inward challenge and began working on himself. Here is his letter to his False Self.

## Brad's Letter

*Dear False Self:*

*I write this letter to make clear our understanding of what was, what is, and what will be, as we embark upon our remaining journey of life on earth.*

*The past was very much your arena. We have been like a ship sailing through life; unfortunately, our true inner spirit has been silent and dormant, like a ship without a rudder. Thus, it has been difficult to stay the course. I recognize your purpose was to navigate through the winds and the storms, to hold the safest course possible to minimize the damage to our ship.*

*While we seldom traveled where we would have chosen, you did a wonderful job of keeping our ship intact, looking good, and disguising the fact we had no rudder, and for that I am extremely grateful. You steered us to wonderful places, to many great experiences. We gained knowledge and talent, and we accumulated growth and wealth along the way.*

*Now, though, our ship needs a retooling. We are lowering the rudder, and our course will be a conscious one. You see, I do have the inner strength, the virtues of a good man, enough wisdom to make good and intelligent decisions, and when problems occur I **can** navigate through them. We do not have to avoid or fear uncharted waters. We do not need to fire our cannons first to survive our encounters. We do not* *need to struggle to control the ocean, because I can control us with the guidance of our rudder, my inner strength, my true being.*

*So you see my friend, I appreciate your watch, but it is my ship and I choose to sail it into the ports of our future. Sure, you will stay on as first mate. I am sure you will have your say about how to do things. I kind of think that will be to fill your needs your way. But that does not seem to work so well where we are today. While the needs are real and a course needs to be charted, a new captain has a dream to put that ship on a course more beautiful, more powerful, and more graceful than ever before. I have a dream of recognizing the beauty and the miracles of the land and sea, to breathe deep the clear air of life and to*

> *smile, knowing I have done it well, no criticism, no regrets, no anger, just a wonderful time spent being the best I can be. Goodbye, see you!*
>
> *Brad*

After the inner work Brad did, his wife began to change and their marriage improved.

The following is an example of my own letter from my True Self to my False Self.

### Author's Letter to False Self

> *Dear False Self:*
>
> *It's time for me to create a new life, to challenge my imagination, to start believing in my capabilities*

and being <u>*Who I am*</u>. *In this dialogue, I am giving my True Self life and I know my experience of life will change for the better. It is self evident that I will grow, and with growth comes change. You no longer need to protect me from this natural process.*

*I see now how you get me into trouble. I am writing to you because I am displeased with the way you continually downgrade my needs to other people. That has actually caused great problems in relationships in my life. Because of you giving up my true voice to accommodate others, my own needs could not be met.*

*You have diverted me from Who I Really Am. The teachings of the church you learned as a child were filtered through the outside world's interpretations of*

*God. People throughout the ages have made God a male sitting up in heaven who would take care of you or punish you if you made a mistake. You've just been living by reacting to life and to other people's ideas of how you should live. All those old beliefs are just that—old ideas passed down through hundreds of generations and relied upon because of the fears inside everyone. The fears are caused by the basic fear of God, just as if God were a parent who will give you a sermon and send you to bed.*

*It's time for me to grow up, take responsibility for my life, and realized how much potential I have. You've been so worried about whether this book I'm writing will please people that you haven't tried to publish it. Now that I'm in charge, I am going to risk*

---

*being Who I Am.*

*I know now that making this shift will make you uncomfortable. Trust me on this. When I make mistakes, they serve a purpose, and I will simply acknowledge them and try not to make them again. No Fear.*

*Love always, Jayne*

---

A shift to your True Self's internal dialogue will not be made without the False Self's resistance. Your False Self has acted like a guardian all your life.

This shift will not be a one-time exercise. You are developing the skill of acknowledging, "I'm in my False Self" and the ability to shift into your True Self. You can utilize this shift for the rest of your life, making it possible to live the majority of your life in a

True Self state of mind. When you decide to shift from your False to your True Self for the first time, you will start a chain of events that will change your life because you will now know how to source internal power. For this shift, know that when you decide to release your False Self (negativity), more of it will come to light so that you can know and release it even better. You will find yourself continually in situations that generate your False Self's personality, giving you the opportunity to practice shifting.

When you consciously invoke growth and change, you are tempting your False Self to come to the foreground of your life. Your False Self is giving you ways to practice letting go to make you stronger. Are you now strong enough to protect yourself without the False Self's bravado? With each experience you are given the choice or challenge to give in to it. The True Self becomes stronger in the same way a muscle does, with constant use. Each time you are aware of your False Self and challenge it, it loses power and the True Self gains power. With each negative feeling you catch, like jealousy, fear, or anger, you empower yourself. Practice is the only way for your True Self to grow and strengthen.

So when you decide to make this shift and step into your True Self, be ready for challenges. If you can't let go of the negative feelings, you are giving the False Self permission to take care of you and be irresponsible. Usually the False Self will attack you where you are the weakest and tempt you with your addictions. Therefore, the False Self is a teacher and will bring you opportunities to heal when you are in most need. Each time you release an addictive act, you are changing your power source from external to internal.

The relationship between your False Self and your True Self might seem adversarial. You must not let the two get into a power struggle. They are both a part of you and always will be. If you are to be successful shifting, you must be truly ready to give up the patterns of behavior that the False Self has used all these years and get out of this comfort zone of protection from change. There is always a fearful time when you give up a way of living and aren't sure of the replacement.

In the next dialogue, we will spend some time developing the identity of the True Self. When you have the courage to claim your authentic internal power, Providence seems to move up to join you.

Proceed with confidence and belief in the highest part of yourself. There will be times when you change into a False Self state of mind, which will remind you of the person you no longer are.

RESISTANCE: Your False Self is not stronger than your True Self is; it has just been in power for a very long time. It cannot survive exposure. Continue to pump up the True Self's muscle by writing more of what you feel might be your True Self. You might have to guess at first.

INSIDE WINS: What light bulbs have gone on for you in this dialogue? You cannot overcome your False Self by rejecting it or thinking your way out of it. You keep the False Self on your side by leaving it behind you. How many times this week have you moved your False Self aside in your thoughts and gone forward?

1.

2.

3.

OUTSIDE WINS: How are people reacting differently to you now?

1.

2.

3.

CHECKPOINT: When you realize you can't get rid of the False Self and learn to accept it for all it has done for you.

# Chapter Eight:

# Changing of the Guard

---

*Time must be spent in the development of our True Self*

*to be the leader of the False Self.*

---

*I read and walked for miles at night along the beach, writing bad blank verse and searching endlessly for someone wonderful who would step out of the darkness and change my life. It never crossed my mind that person could be me.*

*Anna Quindlen*

Golden Rule

*Others will do unto you as you do unto yourself.*

*Jayne Gardner*

187

The experience with rock climbing showed me I was stronger than I thought, but I still needed an experience to solidify my True Self's leadership.

*When I arrived at the hospital my father was already in his room. He was in the bright spirits of someone who knows they are facing a difficult time and is determined to stay up-beat. My father's cheerfulness was maintained by conversation about other things. We discussed the perils of the stock market and the mornings predicted weather. My father joked with the nurse that he needed to call his stockbroker one more time before they took him away. As they wheeled him away, he called in a cheery, strong voice reminding us to phone his golf buddies and tell them he'd be back for his Tuesday game. I* swallowed my fear about his well being by keeping up a superficial conversation with my mother and brother.

We all eventually ran out of trivial talk and pretended to read the morning newspaper beside the vending machine in the hospital waiting room. After half an hour, which felt like three hours, another nurse escorted us to a room where the doctor could update us on the condition of my father's heart.

It wasn't good news. My father's heart was not working well due to four arteries being blocked. Surgery was recommended for the next day. The doctors felt he could have a heart attack any moment.

I knew my father would be mad at missing his golf game, but I couldn't foresee at that moment the true impact this would have on him. The child in me wanted my father to handle this new challenge like he *handled everything: confidently, cheerfully, with strength, and protecting his family from his fears and anxiety. I felt an uneasy stirring, because my role as daughter and child might be threatened, but my long weeks of writing had prepared me well for the next opportunity to be my True Self.*

*My father's reaction to the impending surgery surprised me. At 76, he knew that open-heart surgery meant the distinct possibility of death. He chose that afternoon to explore his early life and share his fear of the future. He climbed right down off the pedestal and offered me the opportunity to join him in a communion of two equals.*

*My father and I talked about his fears, and I saw his emotional closet door being opened by death's hand. He shared with me some of his past—how he had felt over-shadowed by his older brother, whom his father had always favored. The impending surgery allowed both of us time to talk about some of our feelings about growing up. I said I wished he had been around more when I was growing up. I quieted the Pleaser as I realized I had risked hurting his feelings.*

*My father's reaction was slow. "I was busy doing what fathers do, sweetheart. I never wanted you to have to worry about financial problems or any other problem, for that matter. I did the best job I could to make life easy and safe for you."*

*"I just always felt left out by the relationships you had with my brothers. I feel you respect them more. I always wanted to be a boy when I was little to get more attention from you," I said bravely.*

*In the midst of the new freedom of speech between the two of us, my father leaned out over the edge of the hospital bed and told me he had never known I felt that way. Never at all, he said. He told me that he had missed the birth of my older brother due to the war, but my birth had been different. He had asked our small town doctor to allow him into the delivery room at my birth. The doctor had granted him his wish, although it was not an accepted procedure, as it is now. My father looked carefully in my eyes when he told me about the day I was born. He had been one of five brothers, he reminded me.*

*"When you were born, I looked at your mother and said, "Oh good! It's a girl—a little girl! We have our own little girl now."*

At the end of my life if someone asks me which moment was the most loving, I'll say it was this. The shift that occurred was not so much realizing that my father had always accepted me, it was the startling conclusion that I was never going to feel complete if I kept depending on others to validate me. Society had programmed my father to take care of me in a certain way, and he had done his job. It was time for me to let go of the rope and reach for the next handhold without looking down or up for support. I had to quit looking for approval and support outside myself. I had my father's love inside me, and it would never go away. My job was to continue to feel that love.

After my father came out of recovery and was back in his room, an incident provided me with the chance to try out my new true self again. Was there a practical application of these exquisite inner feelings to solving life's problems? The problem came in the form of a threat arising from the hospital staff's poor treatment of my father.

*One of the ICU nurses, according to my Mother, was rude and uncaring in nursing my father on her 12-hour shift. My father was not having an easy recovery, and my two brothers and I calmed my Mother with excuses about the nurses being over-worked. But when the nurse lost her temper with my mother and ordered her out of the ICU, I decided her treatment was out of line. During the next visit, my brother and I walked into the ICU station to find the nurse yelling at my father, who was sedated, talking irrationally, and restrained.*

*Anger cleared the way for my True Self to show the world that she was now a free and independent woman. Rage made the connection for me from inside presence to outside reality. It was not a scary feeling; it was a knowing, steadying sensation, like an anchor thrown overboard for my soul.*

*Neurons began firing off. I saw the blue sky in the plate glass window as my brothers and I discussed the situation in an adjoining room. My kind father, who had spent his early youth soldiering for my brothers and me and over-working so that I might have more, was suffering at the hands of an unthinking, uncaring hospital employee.*

*I walked out of the conversation with my two brothers and without a moment's hesitation went through the large ICU doors stating that visiting hours were over. Rules went flying out the window. My True Self walked steadily and calmly up to the nurse's station. My courage almost left me when I spied a doctor standing close by. Doctors symbolized as much outside authority as did ministers in my False Self's beliefs. But my inner strength won out here, too. I knew my True Self had taken over completely.*

*The startled nurse came fussing around the desk to shoo me back to the waiting room where I belonged. I did not comply with her directives. My True Self's voice was clear, steady, and strong as I calmly requested a room to speak privately with her. She immediately complied.*

*In a very clear assertive voice, I told her how I would like to see my Father taken care of while in ICU. I told her one of my immediate family members would be sitting in the room with my father at all times to be assured that he was receiving good care. "Yes, I understand" was the nurse's only reply.*

*My shoulders were back so far that my spine hurt. The area between my heart and my stomach had lengthened until I had the posture I'd always coveted in others. I felt more full of myself than I'd ever felt in my life.*

*With this newly found inner presence, I walked back into the waiting room to lead my family in our mission to be at by my father's bedside until he was out of danger. I could plainly hear my own inner voice now and wanted to stay in touch and never lose it.*

I suddenly remembered the booming authoritarian voice of the minister—the voice of a patriarchal church and of God the Father. His voice had left me vulnerable and doubtful. Now I realized that voice had silenced mine but in the end had given voice to my inner authority. I was grateful for the experience and respectful of the patience it took for me to look back and pull it out of my history. My own self-discovery work was paying off.

In this dialogue, you will have a chance to pump up the volume of your True Self's voice.

---

### **Self-Discovery Dialogue Eight**

The Development of your True Self

---

*If we leave our father's house, we have to make ourselves self-reliant. Otherwise, we just fall into another father's house.*

*Sue Monke Kidd*

In order to be a strong leader in your inner dialogue with your False Self, you will need to know who you are. Becoming experienced in dialoguing between your False Self and True Self is the highest priority in your life, as it leads you to begin living your life in your highest self. It will demand that in your morning writings you practice writing from your True Self. To bring out your True Self, start your sentences with phrases like "I am," "I feel," and "I want." Replace the droning of your False Self's automatic writing with fresh, consciously chosen words to illustrate your identity. Here is an example of my True Self's writing:

## Author's Journal

*I continue to find my voice and tell my story. I am identifying what I value in life. Who am I anyway? What do I believe? I am a person who touches the deepest part in people by giving out agape love, thus accepting people unconditionally and without judgment. I am conscious when I am being pulled by the outside world, and my voice is heard when institutions or authority figures seek to control anyone's spirit. When I see young children's spirits trapped by parental expectations, I consciously and kindly express my feelings. I fight evil with love and*

> *break down hierarchical controls. I calibrate my space in the universe with my voice. I live from the inside out, knowing God is at my center. I live in my True Self.*

To determine what is important for you in your creative life, write down your answers to the following:

1. What was a dream you had for yourself as a child? Did you abandon it? When? Why?

   _____

   _____

   _____

2. What if you were given a party on your 100th birthday? Why would your friends and family

honor you? What values do you want to be remembered for?

_____

_____

_____

3. What if someone took something from your identity, your True Self, and you said, "This is not me anymore." What did they take from you?

_____

_____

_____

Next, close your eyes for a few moments. Relax and let go of the outside world. When you go inside, search through your memory bank and find two or three instances where you can remember saying to yourself, "This is it. I am having such a good time right now in the moment. This is what life is all about. I am really happy and fulfilled at this moment."

Let several memories come and go until you have settled on the one that seems to be the clearest. Now write the memory down in as much detail as possible, trying to remember what it was about this time that felt so good to you.

_____

_____

_____

Answer the following questions about the memory. What were you doing?

_____

_____

_____

What were you feeling?

_____

_____

_____

Who was there?

_____

_____

_____

Why do you think you felt so fulfilled?

_____

_____

_____

Cliff's Fulfillment Memory

*Cliff remembered a time in his life when he and his*

---

*wife traveled to Italy to visit some old friends. They were all sitting in a café in an Italian village. A band was playing lively music, and the food and wine were especially tasty. He remembered the jovial and rowdy atmosphere; his friends were joking and telling old stories. His wife offered a toast "Future happiness just as today!"*

---

Some of the values illustrated in this memory are Relationship, Travel, Adventure, and Sensuality.

## Author's Memory

---

*The memory that came to me was when the entire family was at a golf resort. I was driving the golf cart all alone up to the next green to catch up with the*

---

*others. As I approached, I caught the beauty of the late afternoon sun shining down on my laughing family. It was fall, and the sun caught the colors of the leaves. I stopped the cart with a lump in my throat about the fun we were having as a family, the beauty of the day, and my reflection on life at this moment.*

From my golf memory, I ferreted out Spirituality, Love of Nature, and Family as three of my values.

Which values might represent the True you?

_____

_____

_____

When you access your True Self, you naturally exude your true presence. Owning your own internal power is difficult because you have been taught that we should play down our greatness to make others feel good.

What is a True Self state of mind? Being present oriented is distinctively True Self. Focusing on your wins and not trying to correct your faults is True Self living. Being true to your values and not being influenced by external forces is living your authenticity. Being aware of your gifts and making a contribution to others as you see fit is True Self living. Being present oriented and focusing on your success (wins) fosters the shift from False Self to True Self.

As you become more comfortable with your True Self's identity, you can progress in your morning writings to dialoguing between your False Self and True Self, exchanging ideas and rethinking future decisions based on your new-found personal values. Never forget to acknowledge your False Self by spending some of your writing every day expressing that side. I always like to end with my True Self's voice.

RESISTANCE: The greatest resistance my clients experience is accepting their own gifts and talents. I encourage you to own your own greatness and take responsibility for what you can offer the world as a result.

INSIDE WINS: What, in this dialogue, have you discovered about your True Self?

1.

2.

3.


<u>OUTSIDE WINS:</u> How could your True Self change other people?

1.

2.

3.


<u>CHECKPOINT:</u> Self-understanding and acceptance.

## Chapter Nine:

## Finding the God Within

> *When aligned, our two parts have unlimited power and*
>
> *we are the holographic reflection of God.*

*I was searching all about,*

*Searching for life and peace,*

*Thinking they were found without,*

*Still, I could find no ease.*

*But the Christ who dwells within me*

*Heard my despairing cry,*

*Said, "Why seek outside of thee,*

*For here am I."*

*Howard E. Smith*

Through my writing over the months and years, something was changing inside me. The talk with my father and the realization that he had always wanted a girl was the last piece of the puzzle to my acceptance of my True Self.

*"Where is God, anyway?" I asked my mother. As a child I had always wondered where God lived, but I had not had the nerve to open my mouth about God or religion. I wanted to ask a million questions about heaven but knew when to be quiet.*

*I fondly remember lying on a quilt one summer night in Texas when I was eight yours old. As kids, we used to yank the nicely folded quilts out of my mom's linen closet and haul them outside. Our mission was to stare up into the stars and see the pictures there. We held very serious conversations about the mysteries of the world. But this night I kept wondering about why God was so far away in heaven.*

*"It's hard to get to him up in heaven," I complained. I had felt so empty to know that God was way up there and that I was way down here and alone—at best, a poor, long-distance connection.*

*I recalled my mother telling me that night that she believed God was inside us. Wow, what a concept! She revealed that to me as if it were to be kept a secret because some people might not see it that way. Still, she gave me permission to think of God inside of me, maybe even as part of me—the best part. That night, long ago, I took comfort feeling that God was inside me.*

My Pleaser had been wrong all these years, thinking my father had favored the boys. The Pleaser has been wrong about a lot of things and had created within me false beliefs and self-doubt. But the bigger error had been to think God would guarantee me a ticket to heaven if I read people's minds and tried to be what pleased them. It had started with trying to please my father and had ended with trying to please a minister. Now I sympathized with the Pleaser's real intention: to please God.

As I shifted into the acceptance that God was inside me as well as in the heavens, I behaved differently. If God was inside me, I could stand up straighter and respond differently to my father. I could express my opinions to him about relationships, money, and my business. I could give my opinion about his medical care, the upbringing of my nieces and nephews, and what might happen in the stock market.

As the relationship with my biological father changed, so did the relationship with my heavenly father. I know that my childhood concept of God was a care-taking father much like my own. My relationship with this God had left me with few choices. God was a man and stronger than I was. The incident with the minister mirrored my relationship with God. I saw the minister as more powerful than I. I had played by the patriarchal rules and suffered.

Taking God down from heaven challenged me to define what my personal view of God really was. I had been dependent on my image of God as our father. Maybe I wanted to stay a child for life. The externalization of God actually separated me from

God. A new concept of God emerged—different than what I was taught as a child. My traditional concept of God no longer served me as an adult.

I felt God was on the inside of me as well as everywhere else. I made a mental shift, taking God out of the sky and putting God within me. I decided God could be a feeling or a presence in my consciousness. I believe God is everywhere in the form of love. I equate this presence of a God inside me to a True Self state of mind. This True Self is my highest self and is connected to a universal power—so great, my feeble little human brain can't even conceive of its magnitude. The only thing holding me back from this incredible internal power is the presence of the Pleaser's self-doubts. These self-doubts created this need to please others and thus disregard the God inside me.

But with this understanding of the truth about God being my highest self came an awesome sense of responsibility. If God was not a separate entity and was inside me, then developing my potential was my purpose in life. Every thought and feeling I had was a direct representation of God. It began to seep in. My personal thoughts and feelings were infinitely powerful—enough so to create and manifest in my life and the world. The power I'd been searching for all my life and thought only men possessed had been inside me all along. Like the Holy Grail, it had been right in front of me as I searched the world feverishly.

The word "responsibility" kept echoing in my head. It implied responsibility for every thought and feeling I had, including the responsibility to keep my thoughts creative and loving about others and myself. What happened if I carried judgment in my heart? Does that mean I create judgment out in the world? If God was on the inside, then everything begins inside me, as it does in everyone. I must learn to be vigilant of every thought, to catch and throw out the negative ones so God could live in me.

I must take responsibility to continue to work on my inner life to allow my True Self to exist, to live, to love, and to create. I remembered hearing the Dalai Lama say, "My religion is kindness." I associated the word "kind" with my biological father. Could I be kind to myself? Could I stand up for my own truth? Could I dare to be authentic out in the world? Could I always be kind and still not worry about pleasing others? I had

217

stripped away the old brittle layers to expose a tender green soul within—the True Me.

I seemed to settle into myself and receive what was rightfully mine: peace and contentment. Instead of trying so hard to make it be right, I simply let it be right. I made room for God.

Paradoxically, as I let go and surrendered my urgency to please for a quiet acceptance, everybody else began to change. My father was more pleased with me. My friends called me more. My brothers were more interested in me. My children became stronger and gave me more love. People respected me more. Maybe I had just turned on the receiver and heard what had always been coming in. The static of the Pleaser's interference was gone, and I could receive more. Maybe they seemed loving and accepting of me because my heart was emptied of all the resentment the Pleaser had stashed away.

As I focused on my relationship with myself, my urgency to find a life partner ebbed. Instead, I concentrated on being my highest self. Interestingly, I was attracting the kind of person I desired. I found the right partner because of the focus and diligent work on my relationship within.

Life suddenly eased up for me. The problems in my life were solved when I lived according to my True Self philosophy: <u>Everything Begins with You</u>. My relationship issues changed when I realized that any problem I was having with other people was mirroring my state of mind. I had the power to make relationships work as long as I focused on my relationship with myself. My money became less difficult as I changed my relationship with it. I was learning to manage my money instead of allowing it to manage me. My health improved as I came to respect and take exquisite care of my body. I chose carefully what I ate and drank, exercised, and prayed daily. The prayers were directed to the God inside me.

My career flourished as I taught this simple truth to others. I changed from counseling, which emphasizes fixing what's wrong with people; to coaching, which emphasizes what's right with people. I was helping people uncover their own True Selves, with the Self-Discovery Solution. It was so easy going to work now, to coach people about relationships. First, I discovered almost everyone was in their False Self state of mind when they walked in the door. They were critical of themselves or others and were usually trying to change some circumstance or person with great diligence.

As soon as I heard them describe relationship problems, I realized that who and what existed in their life was no accident. As in my life, their circumstances were a mirror of what was going on inside. I would begin by working with them on the relationship they had with themselves—introduce them to their False Self. As soon as they embraced this concept, started to meet their own needs, and pumped up their True Self, they would experience a change in their relationship with others. All I had to do was focus them on the inside, to help them realize the enormous power they had to live more fulfilling relationships by changing their relationships with themselves.

As for myself, I was religiously faithful to my morning dialogue, settling the False Self down and receiving my True Self's more positive perspective of life. As will happen, I got off the inner path of truth at times. Most often, this occurred when I attempted to discount or totally reject my False Self. When I fell into my old patterns of pleasing, I would soon be reminded that my False Self was offering me an opportunity to discover new ways to grow and change. Fulfillment always returned when I stepped back on the inner path of listening to my False Self and True Self for change rather than to the world outside or other people. It wasn't always easy. It was often hard work, but when I did the work, change seemed simple and at times, magical. If I did my work, my dialoguing, I could stay connected to my highest self, the power of God inside of me. As long as I was faithful to the morning time, the self-love and contentment came. God really was on the inside. As I nurtured this experience of the God inside, my own internal voice grew stronger and it became easier for me to hear God's voice.

This is the inner power that changed me, that will change you, that can change other people, and can change the world. Stay open to the possibilities.

*He that is within me is greater than he that is within the world.*

*Joel Goldsmith*

In the following dialogue, continue developing your relationship within.

---

### **<u>Self-Discovery Dialogue Nine</u>**

Realizing God is on the inside

---

*Jesus answered them: Is it not written in your Law,*

*"I have said you are gods"?*

*John 10: 34*

The dialogue between your False Self and your True Self will continue forever. As you accept the leadership in your True Self, you will become aware of the unlimited possibilities of who you can ultimately become.

Spend some of your writing time in the morning clarifying what you think the highest version of yourself is like. Other dialoguers have associated this with their view of God. You might take this turn naturally or choose to keep your writing clear of any references to God. For myself and others, it is helpful, so if inclined, write down all the beliefs about God you picked up as a child. Then write about your concept of God.

Here are some statements about my evolving concept of inner godliness:

Author's Statements

| My outside view of God was: | My inside view of God is: |
|---|---|
| *God is like an authoritarian parent* | *God can be a feeling, a person, or a concept* |
| *God punishes me for* | *God is always unconditionally* |

| my mistakes | accepting of me |
|---|---|
| God rewards me when I do good | The answer to all my prayers can be found through listening to the God inside me. |
| God makes choices for me | Sometimes the answers are difficult to understand because of the limits on my thinking. |
| God wants me to fear him | God is greater than anything I could imagine |

| | |
|---|---|
| *God is a man sitting in heaven* | *God is an inner state of being* |
| *God is more powerful than and separate from me* | *God is a co-creator with me. Together we can do anything* |
| **God is on the outside** | **God is on the inside** |

I believe God to be ultimate, unconditional love and acceptance. I believe God is providing me with everything I need and want and is prospering inside me. I believe God has given me certain gifts that I am responsible for sharing. I believe my life has a divine purpose. I believe living authentically is practicing the presence of God inside me.

What do you believe about God?

_____

_____

_____

Your final writing assignment, when you are ready, is to write to <u>your</u> God—connecting your True Self to your version of God. By doing this you will automatically strengthen your True Self as well as surrender your False Self to the God within you. You might be surprised, as I was and many of my clients have been, that this surrender allows you to hear your True Self better and to receive responses from the highest part of yourself.

Here is an example of my dialogue to my True Self, which I equate to God.

## Author's Letter to God

*Dear God:*

*I (False Self) made a horrible mistake today, and I am confused and upset about what to do about it.*


*Dearest Jayne:*

*When you are feeling down, fearful, and doubtful, it is your False Self attempting to teach you an important life lesson. You are always pleasing to me. I don't intend life to be so difficult. Stay close to your highest thoughts today. I believe you can do it.*


## Drew's Letter to his God

*Dear God:*

*With quarterly review at the office, golf lessons, the need to organize work, to do so many things, I feel remiss and neglectful. I am trying but not measuring up. I'm devoting too much attention to work and not enough to my morning writing, family, and my own fun.*

*Please help me with my relationship with my wife. I want to do the right thing. Time is short. I want to call my daughter and have an intimate conversation with my wife. Please help me. I want to do the footwork and leave the control in your hands.*

*Drew*

*Dear Drew:*

*I hear your plea. I will be with you today. Do your*

---

*very best and trust that your highest self will unfold, as I know it will.*

*You never give up. You have been diligent and consistent. I am proud of your progress and your personal growth.*

*Love,*

*God*

---

I hope that you will devote thirty minutes of your day to writing. Be cautious always of the world triggering False Self thoughts. By doing this dialoguing activity regularly, you will bring your highest self into being. Any of us at any time can acknowledge the highest part of us, find God inside us, and get answers when we listen. The dialoguing can provide the structure with which to hear God's voice.

I see this inward expression carrying us outward into our rightful place in the world. Stay faithful.

RESISTANCE: Your False Self might greatly resist the idea that God is inside you, because the results will be you will have to take responsibility for using your gifts.

INSIDE WINS: What are the discoveries you are making about your greatness?

1.

2.

3.

OUTSIDE WINS: How is your world changing as a result of your internal discoveries?

1.

2.

3.

<u>CHECKPOINT:</u> Connecting with an internal higher power.

# Afterword

> *The concepts in the Self-Discovery Solution are the result of my integration of ideas from many authors.*

The function of prayer is not to influence God, but rather to change the nature *of the one who prays.*

*Kierkegaard*

In the time following the personal crisis described in Chapter One, I sought out truth and understanding of myself from several sources. Most of the ideas in this book originated from the work of the spiritual leaders I studied.

My graduate study established the theoretical foundation for this book. During my internship in family therapy, I was attracted to the work of Alfred Adler. In sorting out the patterns of my childhood, I used Adler's concepts of Early Recollections and Family Constellations. Adler believed that if children were over-indulged or pampered, they were likely to develop misguided fictions (beliefs) about life, and that these beliefs frequently took the form of inferiority and helplessness. From this study I determined my own feelings of dependency could be traced to a baby-boomer heritage of overprotective parents who sought to insure for their children the good life they had never experienced due to the Depression and World War II.

I credit several people for the philosophical construct of shifting from an external to an internal locus of control. When writing my dissertation, I first studied Julian Rotter, a psychologist who determined that externally located or motivated people believed that fate or God controlled or acted upon them. In contrast, those with an internal locus of control saw themselves as actors or creators in their lives. I decided I wanted to be internally located, but it took the crisis with the minister for me to begin to source from within.

A colleague then introduced me to Caroline Myss's <u>Anatomy of the Spirit,</u> which helped me describe the shift that I wanted to make. I was fascinated that what she suggested was what I had been trying to do in my own life. It was a shift from accepting victimization from an external source that is dictated by outside influences such as the media, political leaders, parents, institutions, and bosses to embracing an internal authority, which is exerted by our own choices. These choices connect us to our True Self.

To develop an internal spirituality, I turned to Gary Zukav's <u>The Seat of the Soul.</u> Zukav mentions situations that shatter our spirits and poison our True Self. We take on a False Self or a personality to protect or cleanse us, but it actually separates us from our truth. For example, he mentions non-forgiveness of self and others, dominance and oppression, emotional pain, irritability, and being lied to or lying as situations that poison our True Self and destroy its strength. He felt the establishment of false beliefs increases separation from our True Self.

Zukav called the two parts of us the personality and the soul. I call the same parts the False Self and the True Self. I learned from Zukav that balancing the two was the key to shifting to internal control, not the power struggle I had first surmised. I referred to Carl Jung and Alice Miller when determining the basis for the False and True Self.

Using Julia Cameron's method of automatic writing, I wrote down my two selves' automatic thoughts. The False Self's voice was dominant, but I could hear my True Self's voice in my writing and thus eventually brought it into my consciousness. Zukav said that the key to internal peace and balance is to stay conscious of both voices. Like Carl Jung, he argued that the False Self must not be responded to with judgment or avoidance but be recognized as a voice indicating how one can heal.

By bringing this negativity into my consciousness, I could take away its power. Through dialoguing, I embraced the ugliness of my False Self and learned to accept it unconditionally. I realized I had created it as a protection from emotional traumas. I gradually let go of the anger I felt for the Pleaser and finally, others.

Awareness is the key, according to Zukav. The True Self remains distant if we are unaware of our False Self, because a continual dialogue between the two occurs, even if it is outside of our awareness. If I am unaware and unable to recognize which part is talking to me, I remain unconnected to my True Self or soul, and it has to exist in a vacuum. If I hear both voices, I can make choices. Because I had been unaware of my False Self's voice, it took a crisis to get my attention so that the necessary guidance could be given to me. That would not have been necessary if I had had contact with my True Self's voice.

My False Self represents the information other people have told me about myself, others, and the world. It is the major teacher for my personal growth. That's why I learned to appreciate its function. It has been, after all, because of the antics of my Pleaser that I learned many life lessons. Before I could access the authentic power my False Self offered me through these lessons, I had to surrender to its teachings or listen to my inner dialogue more.

Zukav postulated that before I could reach my True Self's divinity and peace, I would have to let go of my need for external power. The False Self just kept giving me crisis after crisis to teach me to let go of what I perceived I most needed: love from without, material objects, a dynamic career, and addictions. My

False Self just kept giving me failure after failure to get my attention.

Zukav feels the False Self is a tool of the soul or the True Self and is neither positive nor negative. I just chose to learn from fear and doubt rather than wisdom. He states that becoming aware of the False Self and its way of teaching allows us to choose another way to learn—through wisdom rather than fear.

This study of Zukav's spiritual psychology made clear to me the difference between my two selves and the value of both. More importantly, through dialoguing I learned how to shift from my False Self state of mind into a True Self. I no longer need to learn from fear and doubt. I can learn through wisdom rather than pain. I saw that love from a power outside myself, other than God, will never give me peace. Through this realization, I found the key to develop the dialoguing technique I have used in this book and in my own life.

# Definition of Terms

*In this section I have defined some of the terms I have used in the Self-Discovery Solution.*

**Art of Inner Dialogue:** Talking in writing and aloud between your False Self and your True Self.

**Boundaries:** Actions used to protect the True Self and provide enough space for its growth.

**Checkpoint:** The necessary requirement before you may proceed to the next dialogue.

**Code of Values:** Your True Self's priorities related to time, money, and energy.

**Distractions:** Tolerations; addictions.

**Emotional Charge:** A strong hangover feeling after an upsetting external occurrence, usually associated with past anger.

**False Beliefs:** Unconsciously held beliefs, which are usually established in childhood.

**False Self:** Your external voice, ego, personality, shadow.

**Highest Self:** Your True Self; your soul.

**Inside Win:** Changes you make within yourself— inner shifts, insights, or habit changes.

**Needs:** Something we must provide for to become our True Self.

**Outside Win:** A positive change that happens in your outside world and in your relationships with others as a result of you changing.

**Purpose of Dialogues:** A summary of the mission you must accomplish in each dialogue.

**Resistance:** The subtle and not so subtle actions of the False Self to sabotage your potential for moving forward.

**Shift:** The gradual process where the True Self becomes more powerful than the False Self.

**Trigger:** An event in the present, which unconsciously reminds you of a past event, and may place you in a past feeling state of mind.

**True Beliefs:** Consciously chosen beliefs related to your Code of Values.

**True Self:** Your internal voice, soul, highest self.

**Win:** A True Self state of mind, which focuses on your positive progress, versus focusing on negatives or regrets.

*Jayne Gardner, Ph.D.*

# References

> *I have chosen to be influenced by many of the following leaders in the development of spiritual psychology.*

*There is a continual interaction between your personality and your soul.*

*Gary Zukav*

**Dialogue #1** Cameron, Julia, <u>The Artist's Way.</u>

Steinem, Gloria, <u>Revolution from Within.</u>

Ferguson, Marilyn, <u>The Aquarian Conspiracy</u>.

Greene, Robert, <u>48 Laws of Power</u>.

Gawain, Shakti, <u>Creative Visualization.</u>

Newton Poling, James, <u>The Abuse of Power: A Theological Problem.</u>

**Dialogue #2**   Miller, Alice, <u>The Drama of the Gifted Child</u>.

Goleman, Daniel, <u>Emotional Intelligence.</u>

Bradshaw, John, <u>Homecoming.</u>

Moore, Thomas, <u>Care of the Soul</u>.

Bradshaw, John, <u>Family Secrets.</u>

Anderson, U.S. <u>Three Magic Words</u>.

Basco, Monica Ramirez, <u>Never Good Enough</u>.

Zweig, Connie & Wolf, Steve, <u>Romancing The Shadow.</u>

**Dialogue #3**  Zweig, Connie & Wolf, Steve, <u>Romancing The Shadow.</u>

Basco, Monica, <u>Never Good Enough.</u>

Baldwin, Martha, <u>Self Sabotage.</u>

Fritz, Robert, <u>The Path of Least Resistance.</u>

Zukav, Gary, <u>The Seat of the Soul</u>.

Driekers, Rudolf, <u>Fundamentals of Adlerian Psychology.</u>

**Dialogue #4**  Wilson Schaef, Ann, <u>Escape from Intimacy.</u>

Wilbur, Ken, <u>No Boundary.</u>

Katherine, Anne, <u>Boundaries.</u>

Marlow, Mary Elizabeth, <u>Jumping Mouse</u>.

Northrup, Christiane, <u>Women's Bodies;</u> <u>Women's Wisdom.</u>

Pert, Candace, <u>Molecules of Emotion</u>.

Tschirhart, Linda and Donovan, Mary Ellen, <u>Women and Self-Esteem.</u>

**Dialogue #5**    Myss,Caroline, <u>Anatomy of the Spirit.</u>

Masterson, James, <u>The Search for the</u> <u>Real Self.</u>

Pert, Candace, <u>Molecules of Emotion</u>.

Napier, Nancy J., <u>Recreating Your Self.</u>

**Dialogue #6**    Vaughn, Susan, <u>The Talking Cure.</u>

Marlow, Mary Elizabeth, <u>Jumping</u> <u>Mouse.</u>

Redfield, James, <u>The Celestine</u> <u>Prophecy</u>.

Dyer, Wayne, <u>Manifest Your Destiny.</u>

**Dialogue #7**   Csikszentmihalyi, Mihaly, <u>Flow.</u>

Boldt, Lawrence, <u>Zen and the Art of Making a Living.</u>

**Dialogue #8**   Anderson, Greg, <u>Living Life On Purpose.</u>

Alder, Alfred, <u>What Life Should Mean to You.</u>

Adrienne, Carol, <u>The Purpose of Your Life</u>.

Levoy, Greg, <u>Callings</u>.

Gelb, Michael, <u>How to Think Like Leonardo da Vinci.</u>

Williamson, Mary Anne, <u>A Return to Love</u>.

Ponder, Catherine, <u>The Prospering Power of Prayer.</u>

**Dialogue #9**   Walsch, Neal Donald, <u>Conversations With God.</u>

Butler, Pamela, <u>Talking to Yourself.</u>

Chopra, Deepak, <u>How To Know God.</u>

Goldsmith, Joel S., <u>Practicing the Presence.</u>

Hendricks, Harville, <u>Getting the Love You Want.</u>

Jaworski, Joseph, <u>Synchronicity.</u>

We are interested in your outcomes

We want to hear about your experiences relative to the Self-Discovery Solution. How has your relationship with your self changed? How are you relating to others differently? More importantly, how are others relating to you? What have been the effects on your work and family life? Please send your comments and success stories along with your name, address, phone number and email to:

Innerdirection

2930 Central Drive

Bedford, Texas 76021

Phone: 817-283-7303

www.innerdirection.com

## Self-Discovery Relationship Training

Are you wishing to hire a life or relationship coach? Attend a Self-Discovery Workshop? Utilize Self-Discovery in your corporate culture? Wish to become a coach?

Innerdirection can provide you with your own private coach or you can enroll in more extensive training classes on relationships. The Self-Discovery Solution offers corporate training, classes for single people wishing to find the right relationship, and spiritual classes for further development of the relationship with yourself. We can connect you with our list of certified coaches as well as our latest class offerings.

If you want to develop a career as a coach, Innerdirection offers training for you to become certified as a Self-Discovery Coach.

If you would like Dr. Gardner to speak at your next public event, training conference, or corporate retreat, please contact her through Innerdirection.

*Jayne Gardner, Ph.D.*

# About the Author

Dr Jayne Gardner is the extraordinary personal growth coach, author, speaker, and creator of *The Self-Discovery Solution.* Her gift to the world and her gift to you may not be obvious at first. She will guide you, hold a space for you, and see the True Self inside you, until you make the discovery for yourself. Then it will hit you, she has given you life's greatest gift—yourself—your True Self.

Jayne Gardner obtained her Doctorate of Philosophy in Counseling from the University of North Texas, Denton, Texas, in 1989. She has been in private practice, counseling and coaching, both nationally and internationally, since 1985. Her clientele includes families, individuals, businesses and

corporations.

Printed in the United States
70414LV00001B/1-99

9 781403 318503